FROM NOAH TO HERCULES

BRIAN FORBES

FROM NOAH TO HERCULES

WHAT HISTORY SAYS ABOUT EARLY MAN

Tate Publishing & *Enterprises*

From Noah to Hercules

Published by Tate Publishing & Enterprises, LLC
127 E. Trade Center Terrace | Mustang, Oklahoma 73064 USA
1.888.361.9473 | www.tatepublishing.com

Tate Publishing is committed to excellence in the publishing industry. The company reflects the philosophy established by the founders, based on Psalm 68:11,
"The Lord gave the word and great was the company of those who published it."

Cover design by Kristen Verser
Interior design by Joey Garrett

Published in the United States of America

ISBN: 978-1-61739-428-7
1. Religion / Ancient*
2. History / Ancient / General
11.03.02

TABLE OF CONTENTS

Chapter 1

THE WORLD AS WE KNOW IT

A Description of Early Man

It is a known fact that the earth is 4.5 billion years old. We're not allowed to question it anymore. Everyone who knows their science knows with certainty that the earth is 4.5 billion years old. In fact, they say it so often that people have stopped using "billions of years" and started abbreviating it as *byr.* A billion years is a long time.

Can you believe that of the 4.5 byrs of Earth's history, man has only been man for 200,000 years? It's true. Don't scorn! Scientists, as I write this, are all (nearly) unanimous that man has been around since 200,000 years ago. It's verifiable, experimental, solid, unchanging science! Before about four thousand years ago, our ancestors had trouble being modern. People *nearly* as smart as you, living *nearly* as long as you, didn't build the structures we do. They didn't know how to plant crops. They didn't travel beyond a few miles from home. They even had a hard time creating watercraft sufficient to carry them beyond the sight of land. You may not realize this, but once I say it, you will. Two hundred thousand years is not only a long time, it's a very, very long time.

If you are reading this, you more than likely are of childbearing age. A human generation can be as short as 10 years, but if we are being generous, we would double it. Humans have been around, doing their thing, populating the earth, and figuring out what makes us alive for literally 10,000 generations. That means, just in the human line, you have ten *thousand* mothers and ten *thousand* fathers.

Look at your parents (if you can) and think about their level of intelligence. Think about their ingenuity. Now, think about your siblings (if you can). Are they all as smart as you? I know people who can't figure out how to plug in their TV to get a digital broadcast signal. On the same token, I know other people, my dad and siblings included, who could probably come up with how to make a broadcast signal. It is true that there are stupid people in every generation, but we all know that out of 10,000 generations, we should be able to make a few smart ones too.

Humans reproduce at an exponential rate. As I write this, there are an estimated 6.7 billion people in the world. In 1990, the world's population was estimated to be barely over 5 billion people. When did this exponential population growth begin? Certainly if we were doing this for 10,000 generations, we would have far more people. Do the math.[1]

It turns out that the population exploded because your great-(x 500) grandpa, who was probably about as smart as you, figured out that he could plant a fruit, and that fruit, if watered, would become a whole bunch of fruit within a year or two. It's unlucky for us that the 9,500 generations of grandmas before him, being as smart as your grandma, didn't nag him into looking into this sooner. All it would have taken is one of those guys to come up with an answer and, you know what they say, "Monkey see, monkey do."

But don't you start blaming them for not getting us to the moon sooner! They had the problem of an ice age to deal with. It would be hard to keep chickens during cold winters, especially in the Sahara. They hadn't been introduced to the idea of ranching. You wouldn't be able to figure it out! It's not as obvious when you're hungry. Your children would barely make it through to childbearing age, where they managed exactly two kids per family. (Too many kids means population growth, too few kids means a genetic bottle neck.) Maybe they tried farming clams in a shallow bay. Perhaps they managed a cow or two. I wonder how lizards taste.

Not to worry though. Our family line got their acts together shortly after the 500th generation back. In fact, shortly after they figured out how to plant a seed and water it, maybe the 400–300th generation back, they built commemorative temples and pyramids. They built roads and canals. They mastered the arch and had ships that could sail the Mediterranean. They made music and held festivals. They invented writing and mathematics. Have you read Plato? They finally figured out how to live this thing called life after 9,700 generations of failure![2]

How to Read This Book

The keener of you who are in the crowd will realize that I'm not friendly to the idea of evolution. Frankly, I'm mocking it. Over the last several years, I have become quite good at picking out the problems with the idea. Sarcasm doesn't come naturally to some people. For those who don't easily detect it, I will try to be straightforward in what I say from here on out.

I also realize that everyone has varying levels of patience and interest in the topics I discuss in this book. I want to accommodate everyone. I believe that this message is one that everyone should hear. This section will help you to skim without missing what you find important.

Almost all of my information (even my interpretations) came, in one way or another, from someone else. I have listed the major sources of my information at the end of this book. You will find that the dates and locations of the early historians are listed next to their names. I advise that you briefly familiarize yourself with the sources. Get to know them a little better before you accept their stories.

The rest of this chapter relates my story. I tell of how I came to this knowledge, not having been trained in science or history. It was interest that drove me. Chapter two answers questions and objections I often get when I call people's attention to the historical perspectives I have discovered. Most of them have to do with science. If you are not interested in science or don't want to take my word for it, feel free to skim the headings. There might just be something there you haven't yet considered. This will end my speculation and summary.

The history, the real evidence, begins in chapter three. I draw from early Greek and Roman historians, who draw from all the histories of the inhabited world of the time. The crux of my book is in chapter three. Chapter four is about the book that started me into this perspective. I briefly discuss the controversy and relate some of the things it says. Chapter five reviews parallel stories to Genesis and discusses why I accept Genesis, not just as history, but scripture. Chapter six is, in my opinion, the most convincing testimony that my thesis is true, and chapter seven is my closing remarks. I do my best to draw your mind to the most important conclusions that come from the acceptance of the historicity of Hercules. Skim and scan this book as best suits you.

I believe the earth is not old (4.5 billion years). I believe it is young (approx. 6 thousand years). I believe that this stands on scientific grounds. I also believe this stands up under historical scrutiny. If this is true, which I hope to show that it is, there are broader implications, and I will touch on those before the end of this book. The early history of man matters in light of the Theory of Evolution.

Please know that I am not considered an expert in anything. People will see my intro in a few years and call it a straw man. People will read the answers I give in the next chapter and call me ignorant. I do not have a problem with those complaints. It is true that some people have never made the claims I mock, and I can't possibly know everything about history, philosophy, or any of the various sciences I draw from. My answer to this is that I don't have to be an expert. I assure you I didn't make up the arguments that I publicly reject. We don't need a degree in interpersonal relationships to have an interpersonal relationship. We don't need to master science to see bad logic. We don't need to memorize Plato to read him. Some of the finer points of the history I discuss in this book can easily be argued by experts. Likewise, any reader can read this history. These are not my words. You don't have to appeal to my authority. If I do my job right, the experts of that age will speak for themselves.

One Man's Journey Toward Understanding

I don't mock the Theory of Evolution because it seems ridiculous to me. On the contrary…

I was an adult before I started seriously looking into the origin of man. There was a conflict between the religion I had already accepted and the history I had been taught in school. Being a kid, I let my loyalty guide me through my adolescence. I knew that the story of the evolution of man was false. I knew, that is, until I was in college. A friend of mine—who went to the same church as I did and someone whom I respected very much as an intellectual—told me that he was angry with creationists. He had concluded that they had to be liars, because they couldn't be that highly educated and still be taken in by the biblical story, especially with all the evidence to the contrary. The conversation we had that day put a fear in me that lasted for many years. I didn't take science in college, because I knew deep down that he was right. I knew that if I looked into the evidence of the evolution of man that it would not only destroy my faith in Genesis but my faith in the Bible (more on this later). Jesus quoted Genesis. My whole worldview would have to shift if I looked at the evidence. So I didn't.

Early in my adult life, I sat down by myself and thought about life. I thought that the most important thing is to find out what the most important things in life are. I decided that those things had to do with the afterlife. If there is no afterlife, no remembrance of what I am doing now, then nothing that matters to me actually matters. Even if I live a horrible life, it wouldn't matter. Without ever having heard of or read Pascal, I took his wager.

Being a good Christian in my high school years, I had some experience with evangelism. Some of the people I talked to were just as zealous as I was about their own beliefs. I faced the fact early on that people have prejudice. I committed myself to be open to the possibility that my parents' religion was wrong, but I carried on with Jesus anyway. I took a religion class, as I believed that making my own would be the utmost in stupidity. I looked at many religions to see if any held more closely to truth than mine seemed to. I figured that if we're not subject to a thinking personality (e.g. god or some variation on that idea), what religion we believe isn't likely to affect our course after death. At least, it isn't any more likely to affect it than what lipstick the mortician adds to our dead lips. No, if we have a destination, I thought, there is likely to be a path that keeps us moving in that direction. That path is paved by someone. That someone must be able to make it obvious to most.

I began to study religions more deeply. I evaluated the major religions first and left the smaller ones for later. I rejected all of them for a variety of reasons. I might have rejected Judaism, if it were not for the fact that I read a gospel again as an adult. I sat down and read the thing from start to finish in one sitting. I laughed. I cried. I was taken in by Jesus' message! Awesome man, he was. Jesus followed the Jewish Law. I couldn't dismiss Judaism or Christianity. I studied them more deeply. In the end, I kept on the path I started on, but this time, it was my own religion.

After deciding my religion and devoting myself to its study, I worked on my understanding of politics. That quest occupied my mind, and I didn't have to think about history or evolution for several years. I figured that if evolution were true, atheism was the most likely religion.[3] If there is no god, there is not likely an afterlife. What difference does it make if I don't believe in evolution? That made it a lot easier to ignore.

It wasn't until several years ago that a group I'm with decided to go to the Institute for Creation Research (ICR) museum, formerly in San Diego. I had thought about the issue a few times in the interim but never looked into any new evidence, since my friend scared me into my position. I had a few plausibility questions regarding the ark of Noah and biodiversity. The tour was okay. The guide was okay. But I had a revelation at the end of my tour. It just popped into my head. How did Noah fit all those two million species on the ark? Obviously, he didn't! (But that wasn't the revelation.)

The potential for diversity at the beginning was far greater than it is now. The first two bears might have had some common traits (such as being brown), but they might have had major differences (such as big and small in the same litter). In ten generations, some litters may have been white, others black. As long as the black and white didn't mix after that, their line stayed black or white, respectively. We went from mutt to pure breed.[93] We have much less potential for speciation now. That same instant, the story of Jacob and Esau came into my head. Esau had hair like a goat. A man having goat-like hair on his arm showed me that there was probably a wide genetic divergence at the beginning. This spark in me turned to flame.

I began to look into the issue for the first time. I went first to the evolutionists' arguments, and then I went to the creationists'. I would flip and flop in my position. First, I thought the flood was local. Then I reasoned my way through the logic of working for years on a ship to fill with animals when they could walk to a higher mountain. This was either divine miracle or it wasn't true in the slightest. I'd have hard questions posed by the evolutionist, then I'd read the creationist answers. I'd read the creationist complaint and then the evolutionist answer. I would try to talk to evolutionists I knew, but with one exception, they were never interested in helping me. I didn't want to spoil the faith of creationists I knew, so I kept it to myself and a very select group of friends. I went to the impersonal debate sites that were run by evolutionists. Those were enough to get me to question if they had any real evidence.

After a long time being in both perspectives, feeling the stress of uncertainty, I called out to the God I had decided to believe in. I asked Him if He means to say by the story of Adam and Eve that He wants to be chosen. I told Him that there's no point to believing in evolution, especially if I can't find the solid evidence that is alleged to be there, and boy did I look! I told Him that I choose to believe Him and His story. At that moment, I felt what people call a conversion experience. I felt like I gained God's favor.

The next day, answers began to present themselves for things that had bothered me for the longest time. Kent Hovind[5] (God help him!) got me started. Doubts that once riddled my mind were squelched. Sites like *scienceagainstevolution.org* showed me that the science evolutionists claimed was solid proof of evolution was actually more pseudoscience than the evidence for Intelligent Design, and that you don't have to appeal to faith to demonstrate it. Books like Ian Taylor's *In the Minds of Men*[6] showed me that this idea was not new. Books like Bill Cooper's *After the Flood*[7] showed me that Noah wasn't a myth. He was a man whose ancestry wasn't only for Abraham's seed, but it was captured in the genealogies of European kings. I told people my findings; I got excited. I started a group that meets to talk about it, but it wasn't until I read a little book called *Travels of Noah into Europe* by Richard Lynche (1601)[8] that I was motivated to write out the history that has always held the key which unlocks the falsehood of Evolutionism.

Why do I say all this? I believe my life was planned well. I hear people say all the time that they have no regrets. I think they say it to console themselves. Well, I really do have no regrets about how I came to my paradigm, and I think others who follow my lead in this will not be sorry for their trouble. Does that mean that I think that I'm anything special? No! Anyone can walk that path. It's just a matter of setting out to do it. Anyone can write a will or put savings in the bank, but only those who decide to will actually end up doing it.

What does this have to do with Noah? We are biased people. We are talking about beginnings. What we accept or reject is largely based on what we have accepted or rejected in the past. I want you to think through your paradigm before you look at the philosophy of those I quote. Consider what you have accepted and why. Compare my journey to yours. If you don't have the right foundation in the beginning, your later conclusions will likely be flawed as well. I want everyone to be right! I really have been living a joy-filled life, and I'm excited about the work I get to do. If you seek peace, I have found it. One necessary part in finding peace was the confidence I was able to put into the scenario for origins I laid out here. I sincerely hope you are able to use my life experience and the philosophy that comes from it to make your life a little better.

I don't think that I'm exceptional. I hardly think I'm worthy to write this book. I do think I have an understanding of much of the debate, but I'm just a slightly above-average intellect that has spotted a gap in what is otherwise a great set of proofs for Young Earth Creationism (YEC). I have been discovering and accepting the truths of YEC for many years now, and, to date, I have not found any debate regarding our written history. All the creationists seem to be over in the science battle, doing a better job than I ever could. I just don't know anyone (apart from Lynche and those who came before him) who has laid out any kind of history from Noah. In short, I saw a need, and I had the means to satisfy it. Hopefully someone better trained in history can do a better job than I did, once the fire is lit in them. Until then though, you'll have to settle for the best I can do, which, if I say so myself, is still pretty good.

Chapter 2

ANY QUESTIONS BEFORE WE BEGIN

Before erecting a new building, we have to get rid of the old one. Since it is such a difficult task, it behooves us to consider why it is that we want to bother. We have to show the flaws in the old structure. Hopefully, once you read the list, you will be able to see the need for the removal of the old and accept the erection of the new.

This chapter is not intended to be an exhaustive list of errors in the predominant historical worldview. It's not intended to have bulletproof conclusions. It is an introduction. Many people have many barriers to accepting the view that our planet is only half a dozen millennia old. This section serves to penetrate some of these barriers. If you already know most of these answers, or you, like my former self, are not ready to give up your childhood bias, skim the headings. I will do my best to make this section one you don't have to live in, as demolition is hardly a craftsman's project.[9]

On the one hand, I want you to believe everything I say, because I think I'm right. On the other hand, I know I don't know everything about all of these topics. How can anyone be an expert in all of these fields during one lifetime? As with anyone who makes a claim, look with favor on things people have evidence for; look with skepticism on those things people say there is no evidence for. If I appeal to ignorance, look into the topic further and let me know what you find. It could be that the answers to all my problems exist, and I just haven't seen them yet. Likewise, it could be that there are a lot of valuable questions in here that people don't have good answers for. You will have to look to find out.

What Is the Number One Reason Why I Should Accept Your Version of History?

Short answer:

Jesus quoted Genesis as history. He claimed the flood happened and fire is coming.

Longer answer:

Two gospels open with a genealogy of Jesus.[10] One takes the maternal line through Mary, and the other, the paternal through Joseph. They establish not only that Jesus was entitled to be king but that he was born into the same problem that all the sons of Adam are. If a man throws out a literal Genesis, he is forced to conclude that even the gospels are not always literal. Jesus cited historical characters out of Genesis, which I will not list for the sake of brevity. Never once did he claim it was only a story. There is also the fact that repeatedly, and I mean over and over, Genesis clearly foretells the life of Jesus.

Take a look at the genealogy of the men before the flood. If you take the meanings of the names (in Hebrew), such as Adam means "man" and Lamech means "to lament" or "sorrow," there is a sentence. It reads as follows: "Man (is) appointed mortal sorrow; (but) the Blessed God shall come down teaching (that) His death shall bring (the) despairing rest."[11] If that wasn't proof enough, we have the parallels in the sacrificial system given to Adam by the shedding of blood for the remission of sins. The sacrificial system is in cultures around the world. You have Abraham taking his "only son" to be sacrificed. Jesus Himself said that the Passover was a symbol of Him. There are many other examples of the arrival of Jesus being prophesied, and it is easily a book in itself. I encourage you to look into this.

This is not a full answer, but it should be sufficient to start your research. Some people find that this proof is evidence enough to take the old building down. They put their confidence in it. Others think that those who put their faith in this alone are blind and gullible. I am putting out more proof for those who aren't as easily swayed.

But the Universe Is Clearly Too Large To Be Young, Isn't It?

Short answer:

A large universe is only a problem if light is fully understood. Light is not fully understood, so don't put all your eggs in this basket.

Longer answer:

You have to remember that they're measuring specks of light! They're tiny, and they're impossible to travel to. In my opinion, this is the most speculative branch of science. It is also my opinion that any evidence they find regarding these specks will not be verifiable. Without having a starship, we only have one vantage point. There are several places where the Bible says that God "stretches out the heavens like a curtain ..." (Isaiah 40:22). If the stars are moving away from us in every direction (as they are presumed to be, because of red shift, or the increased wave lengths of starlight, presumably caused by the movement of stars), then they started moving somewhere around earth. It's a wonderful place to view the event from. The only stars we know the distance to for sure are those we can measure with parallax trigonometry. The distance to those stars could easily be traveled by light in a hundred years. All the rest are too far to be certain.

I imagine that if we can test a speck of light for all sorts of properties, some smart guy could come along and invent something to create that exact kind of light. The Romulans[12] could! (I'm kidding.) It could be that the speed of light is not constant. If time is not constant, I don't see why light has to be (atomic clocks above sea level run at different rates than those at sea level[13]). I'm not a cosmologist, but I have heard a good number of them speak. They admit to having presumptions, every one of which might change the structure or age of the universe. There are too many unknowns to put our eggs in this basket. When I hear young universe creationist cosmologists,[14] I'm convinced that we have a stronger case for a young universe than those who assume an old one.

The most important part of this answer is as follows: even if the universe is old, it doesn't mean that Genesis can't be literally true. This is not something I would quibble about yet. I'd wait until after we've produced a solid case for a historic Noah.

Animals Adapt to Their Environments, Don't They?

Short answer:

No. That's Lamarckism.

Longer answer:

Every animal seems to have its niche. Every organ has its function. There's very little redundancy, and every part is used. Although we do see some adaptation, it can often happen as easily in the first generation as it can over two. What adaptation we see can help the case for creation as easily as it does evolution. We often see organisms from totally different branches of the evolutionary tree with exactly the same function. For instance, we have birds, bats, pterosaurs, flying squirrels, beetles, grasshoppers, lizards, and even flying snakes, all with flying implements. Luck does favor the prepared, but it doesn't seem like it should with so many animals.

You also find animals with the same adaptations and completely different reproduction: mole, marsupial mole, anteater, numbat, wolf, Tasmanian wolf, etc. The difference between them is how they give birth. There are several animals with a bill: ducks, platypus, and duckbill dinosaur. Lots of animals have webbed feet, and even more have tails. Many different lines have sight: trilobite (we presume they were eyes—why?), flies, snails, humans, and octopuses. Lots of animals have horns: rhino, triceratops, bulls, and lizards. Imagine evolving camouflage more than once: bugs of all stripes, cuddle fish, chameleons, and zebras. Poison is purposeful: snakes, jellyfish, ants, spiders—and that doesn't even include plants or microbes. Notice the similarities between blood and tree sap. They ooze out, keeping invaders from invading. They harden when exposed to air but not inside the body. Fingernails! Taste! Hair! Legs! Now if those weren't enough, you have to evolve sexual reproduction several times too: flowers, bees, rabbits! That's a cool trick.[15] [16]

Lamarckism, or the passing of need-based traits to offspring, has been falsified. Bodily changes have never effected change in the offspring—ever! Ask any circumcised man with kids. If I work out, my kid doesn't come out with muscles. If I cut my hair, it has little—wait—no effect on my great-grandchildren. I didn't even inherit my dad's tan. Consider this: Vietnamese have lived near the equator for centuries. It makes more sense to claim that we had the adaptation built in at the beginning, and some lost it through genetics working with time. You can breed many traits out. If traits were inherited because of need, we would have far thicker pads under our feet![17]

Isn't There Physical Proof That the Earth Is Old?

Short answer:

No. Their proof is conclusively false. They're measuring chemicals, not age.

Longer answer:

The main reason that the earth is believed to be 4.5 billion years old is because of radiometric dating.[18] [19] [20] It's the classic math problem where the car is moving along the freeway at a certain speed. You can figure out how far the car has gone if you know when it started. Likewise, you can figure out when it started if you know where it comes from. I don't doubt the math. The question is, do they really know how fast that car is going? How can you figure out a million year half-life in a matter of a hundred years, let alone a billion year one? That's precision![21]

How is it that we know that there are not bursts of deterioration and that the decay is completely consistent? In my experience with chemical change, let's say popcorn, you get one early on, a few more, then a bunch of change all at once, with a few unpopped kernels at the end. I doubt we know the speed. It is assumed that we know how far the car has traveled. In other words, we presume to know how much of an element there was in the sample to start with. If you have ever seen igneous rocks, you will notice that there are distinct color changes and texture differences. There are air bubbles. You can tell by looking that the lava from one area is different than the lava from another. If you can see these differences with your eyes, don't you think there would be differences in composition? It turns out there are. There have been rocks whose "date" did not correspond to the known date of the flow.[22] In fact, every flow that we have historic records for, once tested, has given wrong radiometric dates![23] If this is false, the burden of proof is on you to find the one that worked. I'll be happy to correct myself. The most important objection is this: they are measuring a chemical ratio, not the age of the earth.

Aren't There Too Many Layers of Sediment?

Short answer:

If uniformitarian assumptions were true, then yes. They are not, so no.

Longer answer:

Uniformitarianism is the assumption that the present is the key to the past. It assumes that if we measure rates of deposition today, we can extrapolate into the past to show just how long it took to build up the deposits we see now. Strict uniformitarians will not allow any kind of catastrophe into their reckoning. This assumption is not consistent with what we see in history. Hurricanes, floods, and landslides all take place in a very short span of time and leave disproportionate results. It is unreasonable not to account for catastrophe. It seems like more and more scientists are starting to allow for momentary rapid change, but we have to remember our history. The uniformitarian assumptions that were made at the time of Darwin became the foundation of what we learn about geology today. The geologic column is built on the assumption that each layer correlates to a time in our distant past.

The geologic column is made of sedimentary rock built on granite. Each layer of sediment is of a particular kind of silt, sand, or mud, and it contains certain kinds of creatures. Each layer spans very great distances. Each layer circles the globe and is rarely disturbed by horizontal gaps. You might have one layer that goes unbroken from California to Kansas. The next layer is of a different kind of sediment, spanning the same distance. Nowhere in the world is the geologic column complete from top to bottom.

By the reckoning of modern geology, there are time gaps everywhere in the world. You might have one inch of one kind of sediment and the next inch of another kind. Each layer has its predicted index fossils, whose corpses were broken and battered, not with time, but during their deposition. Now consider the logic of a sandstorm putting down a layer across the whole earth. What else could lay down a layer that spans that distance? Could you imagine a region on the earth that is missing a 100,000 year chunk of time?[24] What would capture animals like dinosaurs and fish? Water with silt is the only way to make a fossil. What mechanism is there to satisfy all these clues?

Well, the current explanation of life and extinction through eons of time doesn't fit well. What I believe works best is a global flood.[25] [26] Thousands of feet of sediment could easily be laid down in a single catastrophe in a week. Mt. St. Helens is often used as an example of this. The sorting of the organisms is also best explained by a flood.[27] The animals that are close to the bottom of the seafloor are buried first and, likewise, are the last to be exposed at the mountain peaks of today.[28] The animals that could run, fly, or think made it to the top layers. If they were buoyant, they wouldn't sink until a little time had passed. Man and birds are rare fossils. Fossils are rare. We have more fossil clams and leaves than anything else, which proves little to nothing either way. Post flood, we have a couple hundred feet of new sediments, locally burying cities with dust or lava, but most of what is laid down is global.

Take the Grand Canyon in Arizona as an example. You have hundreds of layers, as flat as a pancake, spanning miles with no erosion during the laying down of the layer, no roots running through, and no fallen trees breaking the perfectly straight line. And you have a little river at the bottom of the canyon making a likewise tiny *crevasse*-like canyon. Beyond it, there is a very wide canyon. Uniformitarian assumptions would say that this carving took a very long time, but it doesn't satisfy the evidence of such a wide canyon. It seems like the river has no motivation to cut sideways into the walls. It makes more sense that these layers were laid down all at once, and when a natural dam was breached at the brim of the mountain, Grand Lake flowed over the brim, carving the entire canyon in a very short time. Uniformitarian assumptions make the earth look very old, but they also leave a lot of unanswered questions. A young earth and catastrophes fit many situations better.

This topic is more than a single book's worth. Don't take my inexpert word on the subject. Do a little research for yourself. Andrew Snelling recently finished a massive, two volume text on the subject called *Earth's Catastrophic Past,* and I recommend it for showing a detailed, young earth view of geology. See if you can find good answers on both sides. Hopefully you will find yourself in enough doubt about 1800s geology that you can read the history in the coming chapters without scoffing.

Don't Fossils Take a Long Time to Make?

Short answer:

No. They can do it in a lab in far less than a week.

Longer answer:

For a fossil to be made, it takes sediments (any kind of fine, ground minerals) and water to carry them in.[29] You can quickly grind rocks down with water and force. The more sediment in the water and the faster the current, the more rock gets carved out. Then it takes the time to cure the rock. Rock can set in as little as twenty-four hours. They call it concrete. Likewise, stalactites can be made in very short time.[30] Diamonds have been created in a lab.[31] Some of the most spectacular changes on our planet happen with great force, not necessarily with a lot of time. There are lots of examples of fast permineralization.[32] [33]

We See Small Differences in Breeding, and Small Changes Build to Large Ones, Don't They?

Short answer:

Yes and no. Yes, where it matters, and no, where it doesn't. Mutations hurt us.

Longer answer:

I look different from my dad and mom. Most of that has more to do with sexual reproduction than mutation. We simply don't see new traits being created without mutation, which is detrimental nearly every time. Most changes are filtered out by natural selection and by statistics. Imagine spreading one trait through billions of people. The majority of other people's genes would have to be removed from the mix, leaving only yours with your single beneficial mutation. Your mutation would have to be significant too. I can think of hundreds of places where an extra piece of skin would hinder and only a few places where it might help. Mutations are not a sufficient mechanism! They can, at best, affect your own offspring. It makes far more sense to think that a few mutations happened near the beginning and produced the defects that we see today; they do nothing in the population now. This is the difference between microevolution and macroevolution.

There is no use for an eye without a brain and no use for a brain without something to control. Let's take this as an example. For the sake of argument, let's say that brain came first (evolving a brain, simple enough), as it has more potential than an eye. Until it starts controlling something, it's just excess flesh. It's a hindrance to the organism. What keeps the brain from contradicting itself? Why does it communicate with itself? Bad mutations might just as easily survive, so long as they don't keep the organism from getting away from the predator. Likewise, bad habits or function might just as easily arise. Why not hate every time you do something that keeps you or your progeny alive? It's pure luck that we're not miserable all the time. (Well, I'm not.)

The eye just isn't that simple either. What good is a lens without a muscle to adjust it? What good is a clear picture without a way to interpret it? How do you get a clear picture without being able to discern the difference between a fuzzy picture and a sharp one? How do you get the signal to the muscle? How do you feed the muscle? How do you feed the brain? How do you remove death and other garbage? Take out one part, and you have nothing!

This same principle applies to nearly everything in your body. Imagine digestion without teeth. You need a jaw and the muscles attached to the jaw. What would digestion be without the muscles to move the food down your throat? The whole tract is unbroken from start to end, so our bodies are not destroyed by invaders. What good is it if it just rots in your insides? You need acid and enzymes. You need blood to deliver the nutrients. What's the motivation for blood to give up what it has inside it?

Even what is left to consciousness (bladder control) and what is not (removing your hand from a blazing-hot stove) is beautifully designed! And I think this is something we often forget.

You have to be able to develop all these systems perfectly from a single cell. No, you have to develop them in the male and the female simultaneously! This doesn't even start into the likelihood that the simplest proteins could come about on their own, let alone create machines for duplicating themselves. Put simply, the whole thing is impossible by means of chance.

There are books written on irreducible complexity. If you don't see the problem here, it's probably because you don't want to see it. I recommend David Menton's work[34] if you want more and better examples of how we couldn't have happened upon such a perfect machine. It is a gift.

To summarize, adaptation was built in at the beginning. The more we do change, the less we can change. Apart from breeding, there's no mechanism besides mutation to bring about change. Mutation creates mutants. They're not like mutants in X-Men. They are broken, weak. If something in your nerves isn't built correctly, it's debilitating! If any part of our bodies isn't working the same as it's designed to, we are the worse for it. Those mutations are not always filtered out either: our kids are the worse for it too! All natural selection can do is keep the worst mutations from continuing on in our offspring by not giving us offspring. If beneficial mutations even exist, they will be offset by bad mutations, which are greater than 1000:1 more common.

Can't You See the Similarities Between Creatures?

Short answer:

Microevolution versus macroevolution.

Longer answer:

Just think about how many changes have to happen to take the smallest step between creatures. There are much larger gaps to bridge. How did the whale's nose get on top of its head? It's impossible. Convergent evolution[15] shows that similarities are variations on a theme, not evolution.

Things Are So Badly Designed; We Couldn't Have a Designer, Could We?

Short answer:

Are you kidding me? This question defeats itself.

Longer answer:

This floor plan is badly designed, because this other house has a closet at the entry. This shoe rack is badly designed, because everyone knows that cabinets should be made of cedar. We can find flaws in almost anything, especially if we're used to seeing what we're picking on.

By arguing bad design, you are defeating your argument by the question. If there is a design at all, there is an appeal to what "should" be. There is a purpose for the feature. If the feature fulfills its task at all, the design is adequate. Who is to say that adequacy is not the design? Look at the things they say are badly designed. With every example, the job is being done sufficiently. I love my eyes! I couldn't have made me better! Everyone who looks at nature, unless they've trained themselves to do otherwise, when they look at a feature they have never seen before, they will ask, "What does this do?" The question is not *if* there is design, but *why* is it designed the way it is.

So why didn't God give us the speed of a cheetah or the night vision of an owl or the hearing of a dog or the lungs of a dolphin? When there is evidence of failed design, I fall back on two things: (1) We are fallen. Adam was better. We can't take a genetic problem that came out of Noah or one of his grandchildren and blame God. (2) Having one species depend on another is a wonderful design. We can use a dog's nose or figure out how a bat can hear refracted clicks on a cave wall. It's interesting! It's like a well-molded sculpture. We can ask the artist why, or we can admire. I think that eggs cooked with mushrooms in them are a bad design. If you look at the human body as a whole and you see bad design, I feel for you. Your outlook on life needs work.

Can't You Use Brain Chemistry to Explain Everything To Do With Personality?

Short answer:

No, but many people don't seem to get my reasoning.

Longer answer:

It is a great mystery to me, but God keeps secrets. If you are in doubt about it, and you believe that Jesus knew what he was talking about (which I do), read John and discover that he didn't speak plainly to people. He spoke in parables. Sometimes they got it, like whenever you see the Pharisees getting mad, and sometimes it just went over their heads, as with the statements about eating his flesh. I say that to set up for this: you will either understand my point, or it will be hidden from you. I have experienced a lot of blindness with regard to this argument.

Chemicals can't think. Physical reactions are always consistent. They don't do random things. If you add sugar to your cake, it can't decide not to be sweet. Simply because our brains are complex doesn't mean that they should act in a way that isn't perfectly consistent with chemical reactions.[35] If I asked you if you make decisions, unless you're completely biased in favor of naturalism, you will say unequivocally that you do. And it's no surprise that you'd say that, because I do too! You're not ever going to convince me that my choices are not really choices at all. It simply doesn't work, because I can see. A man that can see will not be convinced by a blind man that he can't see, or worse, that nobody can see.

I'm a programmer. Artificial intelligence is impossible. The closest they can come to it is a randomize function, which uses a clock (or something else that changes) to get a random choice out of a list of options. There's no choice there. It's all predetermined, albeit in a complex and unpredictable way. Somehow, people think that if they make it more complex, that it will be closer to choice. No matter how complex this method is or how much brute force "learning" the machine uses, it will never be what I have.

My mom had a near-death experience. I asked her if it was real. She said it was as real as real life. I've heard others say it was more real than life as we know it. They say it's like waking up. Trying to convince them that it was all in their head isn't going to work. They can see. And I know I'm blind and deaf to many things.

Jesus said that demons existed. He spoke to them as though they were separate from the people he was looking at.

I can't listen to the folks who say I don't have real choice. I can't believe those who think that we're just a sum product of chemical reactions and electrical impulses. I can't, because I *know* I have choice. Why would I decide to become blind? Likewise, I will not convince myself that others are blind when they can see. Saying that others can't hear because I can't is pride. It would be an insult to the person that actually has knowledge. It would be a sign of ignorance in me, and at the point when my blindness is taken away, there would be deep shame in having to admit that I claimed to see that they could not see, when, in fact, all I was doing was accusing them without cause. It's better to remain uncertain than to doubt with certainty.

Your Answers Suck!

Answer:

These are not exhaustive answers. I was not formally trained in any of these areas. Most of these were taken from experts I heard at one time or another, internalized, and then vomited out on you. Hopefully it tastes like bee barf—sweet as honey from the comb. If I didn't adequately address issues you have, write me. I have found satisfaction in the answers I gave. There is certainly more than what I wrote. Through the years, I have found problems with the creation/flood model that seemed insurmountable. I found later that the claims against the creationists were only partially true, not true, or had a really good answer that just took a while for me to find. If you demand a higher standard, that's good! We're here, so there is at least one scenario of origins that satisfies every article of evidence. All you have to do is find it. Don't forget to account for the objections on all sides, and please don't let your bias take you over.

I have more questions.

Answer:

So do I! So did I. The more I searched, the more I found. Ask questions of smart people, especially those who study the Bible. If you believe my answers have been adequate, you can ask me, and I'll do my best. I may even add the more helpful questions to my website. And most of all, ask God persistently. Jesus said that if you seek, you will find. (Matthew 7:7)

What Else?

Short answer:

A possible means is not necessarily a probable one.

Longer answer:

Evolution is made up! Sure, the ideas are very old, as we read many of them in the ancient philosophers, but the fact remains that they're trying to piece together a million-piece jigsaw puzzle into a complete picture, only having a few pieces together. The likelihood of evolution is statistically impossible. Everything looks to be fine tuned, from symbiosis to the position of our planet in the universe. Water itself seems to have all the properties that we would need for manipulating chemicals in our bodies. Ice floats. The intention of naturalists seems to be to reject design and purpose on the outset. Don't tempt me, but I bet if I had fifty years and the motivation to do it, I could make up a story about our origins too, piecing together all I know. It might even be convincing. But you shouldn't trust me with it, because I wasn't there. I don't have a complete picture. One piece that the naturalists seem to ignore is history. Were they there? That is the purpose of this book.

Chapter 3

THE WORLD AS THEY KNEW IT (THE EVIDENCE BEGINS)

Philosophy of History

Before we move on to what these ancients thought about their own past, let's talk about why I think I'm qualified to expound on the subject.

There are many types of history. "How was your day?" "Fine." Not only is that history boring, but it's inaccurate. "Did you hit your sister?" "Well, she was taking my toys." That is an accurate and interesting history, but it's not answering the question that we asked. "Have you ever heard the story of the boy who cried wolf?" Not all of what we read in historical books is history. "I clobbered everyone in that tournament!" Some histories are embellished. Well, it turns out that I'm not the first one to discover all these problems with keeping track of the events of the past.[36] If there are errors in recounting the history, you can believe that there are going to be errors in compiling it too. I'm not the first to discover these problems either. Some of the ancient historians of the past realized that there are people who only study enough history to convince the uneducated of their positions.

Strabo, a historian of Rome around the time of Christ, writes that some authors are, and one author in particular is,

> [C]onstantly vacillating between his desire to be a philosopher and his reluctance to devote himself entirely to this profession, and who therefore succeeds in advancing only far enough to have the appearance of being a philosopher; or of the man who has provided himself with this as a diversion from his regular work, either for his pastime or even amusement . . .[37]

Diodorus, a historian of Sicily and also at the time of Christ, has a similar thought. He thinks that there is too much history to write it all down with accuracy.

> For although the profit which history affords its readers lies in its embracing a vast number and variety of circumstances, yet most writers have recorded no more than isolated wars waged by a single nation or a single state, and but few have undertaken, beginning with the earliest times and coming down to their own day, to record the events connected with all peoples; and of the latter, some have not attached to the several events their own proper dates, and others have passed over the deeds of barbarian peoples; and some, again, have rejected the ancient legends because of the difficulties involved in their treatment, while others have failed to complete the plan to which they had set their hand, their lives having been cut short by fate. [...] No historian has essayed to treat of them within the compass of a single narrative, because of the magnitude of the undertaking. For this reason, since both the dates of the events and the events themselves lie scattered about in numerous treatises and in divers authors, the knowledge of them becomes difficult for the mind to encompass and for the memory to retain. [53]

Some things in history cannot be known. What is available is fragmented. Understanding the past is a massive undertaking. He says further, "But since the knowledge of such matters is unattainable by us, nothing prevents those who have the most to say about them from knowing the least, inasmuch as, while plausibility may persuade the hearing, it by no means discovers the truth."[45] Those are strikes one and two against me. Do I have the authority to write this? Am I a credible witness, or do I know only enough to make it appear that I know my history?

Diodorus makes my excuse for me. In one place he informs his reader that the Greeks study various subjects and only bother with history when they are old. Most are distracted by making a living. The Greeks want to be experts and innovators of history.

The barbarians, however, are not interested in making a living by their history. They simply recite it. He said,

> [T]he barbarians, by sticking to the same things always, keep a firm hold on every detail, while the Greeks, on the other hand, aiming at the profit to be made out of the business, keep founding new schools and, wrangling with each other over the most important matters of speculation, bring it about that their pupils hold conflicting views, and that their minds, vacillating throughout their lives and unable to believe at all with firm conviction, simply wander in confusion.

Those who are paid to know it are also paid to innovate. I am not in this for the money, and nobody expects any innovation from me. What I'm interested to do is relay the ignored message of my predecessors. Like the barbarians, this gives me unique qualifications.

In light of the current state of knowledge, we're stuck between knowing a little about a lot or a lot about a little. There's simply too much to know. I would love to have someone that is far better trained in history to write down what early man says about even earlier man. The problem is that, with only a few exceptions, I have not found any who have.[39] [40] The books I have found on the subject have been dealing in the genealogies of kings, only mentioning the connection between Noah's sons and the gods of the ancient world.

I haven't seen any reference to the quotations of the historians that tell why there is a connection either. These are missing links, and bringing them out should help to make the chain of human events all the stronger. I refer you to others to understand the genealogies and the nuances of the histories and the historians. I will communicate the words of the historians themselves, leaving most of the commentary to the experts. By the end, you, like me, will have discovered that there has been a lot of influence by the "Greek philosophers." They seem so intent on their version of events that they miss the plain meaning of the historians that wrote them down. It might also be nice to answer the most important question of history along the way, namely, where we come from.

An Honorable Past

I'm going to say something that may sound a bit outrageous. I was surprised when I first heard it too, but at the same time, I kept an open mind. I hope you can too. The myths of Greece and Rome were rooted in history. Now don't get too incredulous just yet. I'm not the one who made this concept up. You'll find in the coming chapters that all the historians of those times thought the myths were history. It wasn't until later that they were dismissed.[41] Strabo wrote, "[M]ost of the writers who discuss the same topics that Homer discusses, and also most of the various local traditions, can teach us that these matters are not fictions of poets nor yet of prose writers, but are traces of real persons and events."[37] Diodorus wrote,

> For some readers set up an unfair standard and require in the accounts of the ancient myths the same exactness as in the events of our own time, and using their own life as a standard they pass judgment on those deeds the magnitude of which throw them open to doubt, and estimate the might of Heracles by the weakness of the men of our day, with the result that the exceeding magnitude of his deeds makes the account of them incredible.
>
> In the theatres, for instance, though we are persuaded there have existed no Centaurs who are composed of two different kinds of bodies nor any Geryones with three bodies, we yet look with favour upon such products of the myth as these, and by our applause we enhance the honour of the god.[43]

Many today also use the same standard. Is it reasonable to think that because it hasn't been recorded in the modern day that it isn't possible? This idea has a lot in common with uniformitarianism. (See page 22.) Still, sometimes it makes sense to filter out the spectacular, particularly from Homer. Homer was a poet who wrote around 850 BC, and his was the standard text of his day for religion, history, and entertainment. Strabo said,

> Now inasmuch as Homer referred his myths to the province of education, he was wont to pay considerable attention to the truth. "And he mingled therein" a false element also, giving his sanction to the truth, but using the false to win the favour of the populace and to out-general the masses. "And as when some skilful man overlays gold upon silver," just so was Homer wont to add a mythical element to actual occurrences, thus giving flavour and adornment to his style ...[37]

Strabo builds a defense for Homer. He wasn't ignorant.

> Now is Homer really unaware that the west wind blows from the west? [...] In general, silence is no sign of ignorance; [...]
>
> Moreover, the fabulous creations are not, I take it, a sign of ignorance—not even those stories about Proteus and the Pygmies, nor the potent effects of magic potions, nor any other such inventions of the poets; for these stories are told, not in ignorance of geography, but in order to give pleasure and enjoyment.[37]

And he speaks for Hesiod, another Greek poet from around the time of Homer:

> Yet no one could charge Hesiod with ignorance when he speaks of "men who are half-dog," of "long-headed men" and of "Pygmies;" no more should one charge Homer with ignorance when he tells these mythical stories of his, one of which is that of these very Pygmies; nor Alcman when he tells about "web-footed men;" nor Aeschylus when he speaks of "dog-headed men," or of "men with eyes in their breasts," or of "one-eyed men"; since, at all events, we do not pay much attention to prose writers, either, when they compose stories on many subjects in the guise of history, even if they do not expressly acknowledge that they are dealing in myths. For it is self-evident that they are weaving in myths intentionally, not through ignorance of the facts, but through an intentional invention of the impossible, to gratify the taste for the marvellous and the entertaining."[37]

In his book, Diodorus has "discussion of the customs which each people follows and of the reasons why history records many things in connection with them which are entirely unique and are not believed because they are contrary to what one expects ..."[45]

We have seen two reasons why the histories might have been embellished. One being that it gives flavor to the stories. The other is that they're not actually wrong, just unusual. What better reason is there in reporting an event than that it was not common? The third is this:

> He also threw a wall about the precinct and stationed there many guardians, these being men of the Tauric Chersonese, and it is because of these guards that the Greeks invented monstrous myths. For instance, the report was spread abroad that there were fire-breathing bulls (tauroi) round about the precinct and that a sleepless dragon (drakon) guarded the fleece ...
>
> As for these matters, however, it rests with my readers to judge each in accordance with his own predilections. [43]

I don't want to leave this issue without being clear that these two authors were not the only ones to call the myths history. The people they quote called it so. The other authors, whom I quote elsewhere in this book, also state the myths as true. The legacy of these two is that they address it directly. They were in a position to know, being only removed from Homer by a few hundred years.

These guys took history seriously. This is how the ancients rewarded their historians. Pliny recounts: "Berosus excelled in astrology; and on account of his divinations and predictions, a public statue was erected in his honour by the Athenians."[46] Earlier, he wrote,

> [W]hen he [Alexander the Great] found among the spoils of Darius, the king of Persia, a casket for perfumes, enriched with gold, precious stones, and pearls, covered as he was with the dust of battle, deemed it beneath a warrior to make use of

> unguents, and, when his friends were pointing out to him its various uses, exclaimed, "Nay, but by Hercules! let the casket be used for preserving the poems of Homer"; that so the most precious work of the human mind might be placed in the keeping of the richest work of art.[47]

It is true that both Berosus and Homer were more than historians, but they spent much of their attention on history, and they were all the more celebrated for it. And how accurate did these historians aim to be? Strabo said he wanted "to make everything scientifically accurate ..." [37] He also said in his next book,

> [I]t is not necessary to change the reading, for it is old. It is better to lay the confusion to the change of their name, for such change is frequent and noticeable among all nations, than to change the reading—as in fact some do when they emend by changing certain letters.

And just how much did they write down? Not everything. Strabo says,

> For example, wherein would it be proper for the Indian geographer to add details about Boeotia such as Homer gives: "These were they that dwelt in Hyria and rocky Aulis and Schoenus and Scolus?" For me these details are proper; but when I come to treat India it is no longer proper to add such details; and, in fact, utility does not urge it—and utility above all things is our standard in empirical matters of this kind. [37]

So what was relevant? How far did their knowledge reach? Diodorus says,

> For the supremacy of [Rome], a supremacy so powerful that it extends to the bounds of the inhabited world ...
> Concerning, however, every race of men, and all events that have taken place in the known parts of the inhabited world,

> we shall give an accurate account, so far as that is possible in the case of things that happened so long ago, beginning with the earliest times.[48]

And where did they get their knowledge from? Diodorus says this also,

> Thereupon the Epigoni took the city and sacked it, and captur[ed] Daphnê, [...] This maiden possessed no less knowledge of prophecy than her father, [...] she also wrote oracular responses of every sort, excelling in their composition; and indeed it was from her poetry, they say, that the poet Homer took many verses which he appropriated as his own and with them adorned his own poesy.[43]

I don't think they divined or prophesied the histories. They didn't make them up. I think Daphnê was a learned lady, and she happened to be the lady who wrote some of the account that Homer embellished. Herodotus, a Greek historian who wrote about 450 BC, said,

> The Samothracians received these mysteries from the Pelasgi, who, before they went to live in Attica, were dwellers in Samothrace, and imparted their religious ceremonies to the inhabitants. The Athenians, then, who were the first of all the Greeks to make their statues of Mercury in this way, learnt the practice from the Pelasgians; and by this people a religious account of the matter is given, which is explained in the Samothracian mysteries.[49]

They also counted upon other nameless and faceless historians and priests, documents and monuments that are far too numerous to list. We don't have those writings anymore, much less an ability to test their truthfulness. You'll have to take them at face value. Strabo wrote, "But he should take some other things on faith, even if he does not see a reason for them; for the question of causes belongs to the student of philosophy alone, whereas the statesman does not have adequate leisure for research, or at least not always." [37] If the historians we're quoting seem good enough to trust, trust them. If not, I have only to say that after reading them, I found them to have very critical minds. They already pulled out most of the weeds for us, and we might only have a few left to extract ourselves.[50] If you're a bit too picky, you might inadvertently pull out the good and throw them in the bucket with the bad.

You will notice in the coming quotations that pagan polytheism was not only common at the beginning, it was universal. When a nation didn't believe in a particular god, that fact was mentioned. If they didn't revere any gods, they were all the stranger, and the fact was brought out as color on the characters being described. The known world at the time of Strabo, for example, was from England to India, and from Denmark to Madagascar.[51] In all these places, and even in studying these places today, the original religion was that of paganism, or ancestral worship. I will get into why I think this was later. For now, let's wonder at the similarity.

Ancient Perspectives

Discerning the possible origin options is not a hard feat. Either there was a start or there wasn't. Either there was a starter or there wasn't. Either man has life or he only appears that way. Clearly we're alive, so is that life eternal? All these questions were asked since the beginning. Let's start with what has always been the minority opinion.

Philo, a Jewish philosopher around the time of Christ, wrote,

> For some men, admiring the world itself rather than the Creator of the world, have represented it as existing without any maker, and eternal; and as impiously as falsely have represented God as existing in a state of complete inactivity, while it would have been right on the other hand to marvel at the might of God as the creator and father of all, and

> to admire the world in a degree not exceeding the bounds of moderation. But Moses, who had early reached the very summits of philosophy... was well aware that it is indispensable that in all existing things there must be an active cause, and a passive subject...[52]

In other words, it's doesn't make sense to think that something came from nothing. Diodorus contrasted the two possible origins:

> Now as regards the first origin of mankind two opinions have arisen among the best authorities both on nature and on history. One group, which takes the position that the universe did not come into being and will not decay, has declared that the race of men also has existed from eternity, there having never been a time when men were first begotten; the other group, however, which hold that the universe came into being and will decay, has declared that, like it, men had their first origin at a definite time.[53]

First option, everything is eternal. Second option, we have a beginning, and we'll have an end. Some concepts seem novel—until you find out that there are people who have already thought of them. "For there are some persons who believe that there are many worlds, and some who even fancy that they are boundless in extent..." Philo thinks that those who believe this way are impudent.

> And on the fourth day, after he had embellished the earth, he diversified and adorned the heaven: not giving the precedence to the inferior nature by arranging the heaven subsequently to the earth, [...] For he foreknew with respect to men who were not yet born, what sort of beings they would be as to their opinions, forming conjectures on what was likely and probable, of which the greater part would be reasonable, though falling short of the character of unadulterated truth; and trusting rather to visible phenomena than to God,

> and admiring sophistry rather than wisdom. […] [That] no one might venture either through shameless impudence or inordinate ignorance to attribute to any created thing the primary causes of things, he said: "Let them run over in their minds the first creation of the universe, when, before the sun or the moon existed, the earth brought forth all kinds of plants and all kinds of fruits […] needing no one else as his assistant; for all things are possible to God.[52]

In short, God made the plants before he made the sun, just to prove that He could.

If atheism was the minority view, the opposing view must have been powerful, right? Well, let's see. On the origin of man, Hyginus, a Latin author around the first century BC, wrote,

> Prometheus, son of Iapetus, first fashioned men from clay. Later Vulcan, at Jove's command, made a woman's form from clay. Minerva gave it life, and the rest of the gods each gave [s]ome other gift. Because of this they named her Pandora. She was given in marriage to Prometheus' brother Epimetheus. Pyrrha was her daughter, and was said to be the first mortal born.[54]

Diodorus writes in many places that "Eteocretans [and others] were sprung from the soil itself … "[57] Hyginus says of skin color, "The Indians became black, because their blood was turned to a dark color from the heat that came near."[55]

More than being formed of dirt, another story was pervasive. "In order to have a reason for destroying the whole race of mortals, Jove pretended he wanted to put out the fire; he let loose the rivers everywhere, and all the human race perished except Deucalion and Pyrrha." Hyginus continues,

> When the cataclysm, which we call the flood or deluge, occurred, all the human race perished except Deucalion and Pyrrha, who fled to Mount Etna, which is said to be the highest mountain in Sicily. When they could not live on

account of loneliness, they begged Jove either to give men, or to afflict them with a similar disaster. Then Jove bade them cast stones behind them; those Deucalion threw he ordered to become men, and those Pyrrha threw, to be women. Because of this they are called laos, "people," for stone in Greek is called las.[56]

In other flood accounts, only certain areas were flooded. Diodorus wrote,

> For the Pontus, which had at the time the form of a lake, was so swollen by the rivers which flow into it, that, because of the great flood which had poured into it, its waters burst forth violently into the Hellespont and flooded a large part of the coast of Asia and made no small amount of the level part of the land of Samothrace into a sea; and this is the reason, we are told, why in later times fishermen have now and then brought up in their nets the stone capitals of columns, since even cities were covered by the inundation. The inhabitants who had been caught by the flood, the account continues, ran up to the higher regions of the island; and when the sea kept rising higher and higher, they prayed to the native gods, and since their lives were spared, to commemorate their rescue they set up boundary stones about the entire circuit of the island and dedicated altars upon which they offer sacrifices even to the present day. [57]

Diodorus also seems to indicate that there was also a flood that wiped out just about everything. He holds on to the idea that some survived on mountains.

> Of their number Macar [. . .] founded there the city men call Heliopolis, naming it after his father; and it was from him that the Egyptians learned the laws of astrology.[58] But when at a later time there came a flood among the Greeks and the majority of mankind perished by reason of the abundance of rain, it came to pass that all written monuments were also destroyed in the same manner as mankind; and this is the

reason why the Egyptians, seizing the favourable occasion, appropriated to themselves the knowledge of astrology, and why, since the Greeks, because of their ignorance, no longer laid any claim to writing, the belief prevailed that the Egyptians were the first men to effect the discovery of the stars. Likewise the Athenians, although they were the founders of the city in Egypt men call Saïs, suffered from the same ignorance because of the flood.

The Greeks and Egyptians lost their ability to write. He continues in a different vein.

> Upon the death of Cercaphus his three sons, Lindus, Ialysus, and Cameirus, succeeded to the supreme power; and during their lifetime there came a great deluge and Cyrbê was buried beneath the flood and laid waste, whereupon the three divided the land among themselves, and each of them founded a city which bore his name. [57]

It's interesting to me that the land was divided in three. I will mention this again later.

Diodorus' opinion of early man was much higher than the educated elite of today.

> Indeed, speaking generally, in all things it was necessity itself that became man's teacher, supplying in appropriate fashion instruction in every matter to a creature which was well endowed by nature and had, as its assistants for every purpose, hands and speech and sagacity of mind. [53]

Is this the mighty defeater of atheism? If you were going to make up a creation tradition, wouldn't you make it something a little closer to the theory of evolution? At least it would make sense. Who of you would make the story to be that rocks were thrown over their shoulder and became people? Why all the stories about the flood of the world? This religion makes no sense! Clearly, man was not stupid. We're likely dealing with something more like a phone tree, where one person calls two, and those two call six. Scores of generations added and confused their part of the actual story. As you trace this idea from one tribe to the next, you get a better idea of what the original account was. Each tribe contributes a few details to corroborate for the historian the reliability of the record. Keep this in mind as we continue on with the perspectives on the origin of the gods.

Diodorus starts his sixth book this way:

> As regards the gods, then, men of ancient times have handed down to later generations two different conceptions: Certain of the gods, they say, are eternal and imperishable, such as the sun and moon and the other stars of the heavens, and the winds as well and whatever else possesses a nature similar to theirs; for of each of these the genesis and duration are from everlasting to everlasting. But the other gods, we are told, were terrestrial beings who attained to immortal honour and fame because of their benefactions to mankind, such as Heracles, Dionysus, Aristaeus, and the others who were like them. Regarding these terrestrial gods many and varying accounts have been handed down by the writers of history and mythology; of the historians, Euhemerus, who composed the Sacred History, has written a special treatise about them, while, of the writers of myths, Homer and Hesiod and Orpheus and the others of their kind have invented rather monstrous stories about the gods.[59]

I find this exceptional. He says, in essence, that there are two god types. One is eternal (stars, wind), the others were just men who were elevated to the state of godhood. This seems to be the summation of every religion today as well. We either bow to an immutable, immortal, eternal, benevolent God, or we believe that if we're impressive enough, we can become like gods. Let's move on.

How does one become immortal? Diodorus writes about three gods.

> The myth which the Naxians have to relate about Dionysus is like this: He was reared, they say, in their country, and for this reason the island has been most dear to him and is called by some Dionysias. For according to the myth which has been handed down to us, Zeus, on the occasion when Semelê had been slain by his lightning before the time for bearing the child, took the babe and sewed it up within his thigh, and when the appointed time came for its birth, wishing to keep the matter concealed from Hera, he took the babe from his thigh in what is now Naxos and gave it to the Nymphs of the island, Philia, Coronis, and Cleidê, to be reared. The reason Zeus slew Semelê with his lightning before she could give birth to her child was his desire that the babe should be born, not of a mortal woman but of two immortals, and thus should be immortal from its very birth.

This was stated earlier; Dionysus did not always exist. Who else? Diodorus said, "According to the myth which the priests give, the gods had their origin in Crete, and were led by Zeus to Panchaea at the time when he sojourned among men and was king of the inhabited earth."[57] Zeus had an origin. He was a king of men! He says more,

> Beyond the above-mentioned plain there is a lofty mountain which has been made sacred to the gods and is called the "Throne of Uranus" and also "Triphylian Olympus." For the myth relates that in ancient times, when Uranus was king of the inhabited earth, he took pleasure in tarrying in that place and in surveying from its lofty top both the heavens and the stars therein ...[57]

If Uranus was a king in the earth, who is left? Uranus was supposed to be birthed from Gaia, otherwise known as dirt. The Atlantians said that their "first king was Uranus."[45] The Egyptians held that all sorts of gods had a hand in founding their land. Diodorus makes this comment,

> For the Egyptians [. . .] say, Egypt is the only country in the whole inhabited world where there are many cities which were founded by the first gods, such as Zeus, Helius, Hermes, Apollo, Pan, Eileithyia, and many more. [53]

What other traits did these gods have? They took their sisters for wives. Diodorus says,

> When the valour and fame of Dionysus became spread abroad, Rhea, it is said, angered at Ammon, strongly desired to get Dionysus into her power; but being unable to carry out her design she forsook Ammon and, departing to her brothers, the Titans, married Cronus her brother. [45]

Philo criticized those who believed in these sorts of gods.

> Therefore some persons, marveling at the nature of both these worlds, have not only worshiped them in their entirety as gods, but have also deified the most beautiful parts of them, I mean for instance the sun, and the moon, and the whole heaven, which, without any fear or reverence, they called gods.[60]

Interesting! The planets were named for ancient kings.

Hercules was also a man, and Herodotus tells us that there were at least two men that had his name. Most accounts given are of Hercules, the son of Jupiter (Roman), or Heracles, son of Zeus (Greek). These are just alternate spellings for names given to the same people. These other men, also called Hercules, actually had a different lineage:

> The account which I received of this Hercules makes him one of the twelve gods. Of the other Hercules, with whom the Greeks are familiar; I could hear nothing in any part of Egypt. That the Greeks, however (those I mean who gave the son of Amphitryon that name), took the name from the Egyptians, and not the Egyptians from the Greeks, is I think clearly proved, among other arguments, by the fact that both

> the parents of Hercules, Amphitryon as well as Alcmena, were of Egyptian origin. Again, the Egyptians disclaim all knowledge of the names of Neptune and the Dioscuri, and do not include them in the number of their gods; but had they adopted the name of any god from the Greeks, these would have been the likeliest to obtain notice, since the Egyptians, as I am well convinced, practised navigation at that time, and the Greeks also were some of them mariners, so that they would have been more likely to know the names of these gods than that of Hercules. But the Egyptian Hercules is one of their ancient gods. [49]

Note that both the Greeks and Egyptians were mariners during the time of Hercules. Both Greeks and Egyptians trust their sources as accounts of actual events, and they're arguing about details. Herodotus continues,

> Seventeen thousand years before the reign of Amasis, the twelve gods were, they affirm, produced from the eight: and of these twelve, Hercules is one. In the wish to get the best information that I could on these matters, I made a voyage to Tyre in Phoenicia, hearing there was a temple of Hercules at that place […] In a conversation which I held with the priests, I inquired how long their temple had been built, and found by their answer that they, too, differed from the Greeks. They said that the temple was built at the same time that the city was founded, and that the foundation of the city took place two thousand three hundred years ago.[61] In Tyre I remarked another temple where the same god was worshiped as the Thasian Hercules. So I went on to Thasos, where I found a temple of Hercules which had been built by the Phoenicians who colonised that island when they sailed in search of Europa. Even this was five generations earlier than the time when Hercules, son of Amphitryon, was born in Greece. These researches show plainly that there is an ancient god Hercules; and my own opinion is that those Greeks act most wisely who build and maintain two temples of Hercules, in the one of which the Hercules worshiped is

> known by the name of Olympian, and has sacrifice offered to him as an immortal, while in the other the honours paid are such as are due to a hero. [49]

So, both temples had details about Hercules, and they were born at different times. Herodotus makes a distinction here between a hero that is honored after death and a god on Mount Olympus. You will see that this distinction is artificial. To someone who believes the gods are immortal, however, it makes sense that he would see a difference between them.

Before we go too far down this trail, I want to point out that not everything that these ancient historians said was true. Philo wrote,

> It follows therefore of necessity, that what is outside must either be a vacuum or nothing at all. If now it is a vacuum, than how can that which is full and solid, and the heaviest of all things, avoid being pressed down by its own weight, since there is no solid thing to hold it up?[62]

He also said things that might be true:

> [T]he first man who was ever formed appears to have been the height of perfection of our entire race, and subsequent generations appear never to have reached an equal state of perfection, but to have at all times been inferior both in their appearance and in their power, and to have been constantly degenerating...

Again Philo says,

> Since even those who have been born so many generations afterwards, when the race is becoming weakened by reason of the long intervals of time that have elapsed since the beginning of the world, do still exert the same power over the irrational beasts, preserving as it were a spark of the dominion and power which has been handed down to them by succession from their first ancestor. [52]

I agree that a vacuum couldn't hold things up, but it's not a problem with modern science. He says ignorant things. He also says something profound: we are inferior in body to our ancestors. That seems like it is probably true, especially in light of what early man says about earliest man. I agree with Philo a little more than half the time. These statements, as with everything you hear coming out of people (including yourself), should be taken with an ounce of suspicion. They are as much people as we are. Diodorus wasn't perfect either:

> As proof that animal life appeared first of all in their land they would offer the fact that even at the present day the soil of the Thebaid at certain times generates mice in such numbers and of such size as to astonish all who have witnessed the phenomenon; for some of them are fully formed as far as the breast and front feet and are able to move, while the rest of the body is unformed, the clod of earth still retaining its natural character. [53]

Strabo was a sexist and a classist.

> In the first place, I remark that the poets were not alone in sanctioning myths, for long before the poets the states and the lawgivers had sanctioned them as a useful expedient, since they had an insight into the natural affections of the reasoning animal; for man is eager to learn, and his fondness for tales is a prelude to this quality. It is fondness for tales, then, that induces children to give their attention to narratives and more and more to take part in them. [...] But if you add thereto the marvellous and the portentous, you thereby increase the pleasure, and pleasure acts as a charm to incite to learning.
>
> Now every illiterate and uneducated man is, in a sense, a child, and, like a child, he is fond of stories; and for that matter, so is the half-educated man, for his reasoning faculty

> has not been fully developed, and, besides, the mental habits of his childhood persist in him.
>
> For in dealing with a crowd of women, at least, or with any promiscuous mob, a philosopher cannot influence them by reason or exhort them to reverence, piety and faith; nay, there is need of religious fear also, and this cannot be aroused without myths and marvels. For thunderbolt, aegis, trident, torches, snakes, thyrsus-lances—arms of the gods—are myths, and so is the entire ancient theology. But the founders of states gave their sanction to these things as bugbears wherewith to scare the simple-minded. [42]

Of course, even considering their flaws, it doesn't follow that they weren't smart. They certainly had a handle on their culture and the history they were writing down. You have to examine every detail using its proper weight. Not everything that was said about the gods needs to be given truth status. At the same time, they didn't likely say these things without reason. Everyone has to determine just what they are willing to believe, and each person will be believed based on what they have accepted or rejected for themselves. This isn't an easy thing to do, but everyone, in the end, has to take some position. That decision will be the bias that leads you to accept or reject the next idea. It is for this reason that I urge you to be cautious, even of me. Strabo wrote,

> However, even if those who hand down to us our knowledge of the regions under consideration do not agree among themselves, we should not on that account set aside the entire body of that knowledge; indeed there are times when the account as a whole is all the more to be accepted for this reason. [44]

It seems counterintuitive, but he tells us that when they disagree at points, we have more reason to trust them. He supports his claim with an example where three sources point in a particular direction. Two of the sources disagree on the exact location. Because all three agree that the landmark exists, and is somewhere around there, we can trust that it is, even if we don't see its ruins.

With all these authors, and all they tell us, we need to take the time to consider when we need to be doubtful, and, likewise, when we need to be trusting.

The World as Described by Ancient Historians

The earliest people seemed to be unanimous in their beliefs. They had one religion that was everywhere. It was in Libya. It was in Egypt. It was in India. The barbarians all clung to it, and the Persians did too. It is pagan polytheism. They worshiped the things around them, revered their ancestors, and made idols. The nations had common characters with common traits and common stories about their excellence and deeds. Today, we know the names of the gods of both Greece and Rome. Rome conquered Greece, but Greece was more highly regarded for their intelligence, so we remember both. We don't remember Ra or Thor quite as often.

Take a step back for a second. Think about that. Every nation whose indigenous population had its history recorded had people who revered their ancestors, attributed character to their surroundings, and named gods. Now consider this in light of the commonality. The places where writing was developed enough to keep a record at the earliest times (China, India, and the Americas excluded for this book) connect the common gods between nations. The ancient geographers actually tell us which gods were common between nations and which were not. I don't know how many times I read that a particular god was revered in another nation under a different name and in only a slightly different way. It would number in the hundreds.

It's possible to correlate the gods with some of the characters from Genesis, but I'm not going to make an exhaustive and speculative list. I leave that task to you. I'm only going to make a few connections, and I look forward to seeing what others come up with. I hope you don't take to sacrificing pigs to them once you're done.

Herodotus repeats this very interesting story.

> When Hecataeus the historian was at Thebes, and, discoursing of his genealogy, traced his descent to a god in the person of his sixteenth ancestor, the priests of Jupiter did to him exactly as they afterwards did to me, though I made no boast of my family. They led me into the inner sanctuary, which is a spacious chamber, and showed me a multitude of colossal statues, in wood, which they counted up, and found to amount to the exact number they had said; the custom being for every high priest during his lifetime to set up his statue in the temple. As they showed me the figures and reckoned them up, they assured me that each was the son of the one preceding him; and this they repeated throughout the whole line, beginning with the representation of the priest last deceased, and continuing till they had completed the series. When Hecataeus, in giving his genealogy, mentioned a god as his sixteenth ancestor, the priests opposed their genealogy to his, going through this list, and refusing to allow that any man was ever born of a god. Their colossal figures were each, they said, a Piromis, born of a Piromis, and the number of them was three hundred and forty-five; through the whole series Piromis followed Piromis, and the line did not run up either to a god or a hero. The word Piromis may be rendered "gentleman." [49]

Let me just point out that Hecataeus knew his sixteenth generation. Now if that was sixteen back or sixteen from the top, either way, they kept genealogical records for a long time back then. Herodotus makes another telling statement. "Again, on one occasion they determined that they would no longer make use of the foreign temples which had been long established among them, but would worship their own old ancestral gods alone." They borrowed gods. It is also worthy of note that not every ancestor was in the lineage of a particular group. The biggest and first names were common to everyone, but the ones that come later are only useful to the local population. If it was a powerful conqueror, like Osiris or Hercules, the lands they defeated would keep them in mind as they made their sacrifices.

If you're in doubt that they worshiped their ancestors, let me make that point a little clearer. "On the death of Lycurgus they built him a temple, and ever since they have worshiped him with the utmost reverence."[63] Diodorus also makes this claim.

> And since he [Tenedos] governed uprightly and conferred many benefactions upon the inhabitants, during his lifetime he was in high favour, and upon his death he was granted immortal honours; for they built for him a sacred precinct and honoured him with sacrifices as though he were a god, and these sacrifices they have continued to perform down to modern times. [57]

It happened for nobodies. Who ever heard of Lycurgus or Tenedos? Let's see if it's any clearer for more recognizable names. In the same book, Diodorus says,

> Regarding the birth of Zeus and the manner in which he came to be king, there is no agreement. Some say that he succeeded to the kingship after Cronus passed from among men into the company of the gods, not by overcoming his father with violence, but in the manner prescribed by custom and justly, having been judged worthy of that honour. But others recount a myth, which runs as follows:
>
> Now the Giants were punished by Zeus because they had treated the rest of mankind in a lawless fashion and, confiding in their bodily superiority and strength, had enslaved their neighbours, and because they were also disobeying the rules of justice which he was laying down and were raising up war against those whom all mankind considered to be gods because of the benefactions they were conferring upon men generally. Zeus […] totally eradicated the impious and evil-doers from among mankind …

As I said before, the phone tree has broken the story up a bit, but it's clear to Diodorus that Zeus had an actual birth and was an actual king. It is also interesting to note what it says about Zeus (called Osiris by Lynche in chapter four of this book), who waged war on the giants.

Until now, I've been using the same sources. Let's spread the load a bit. Dionysius of Halicarnassus, a Greek historian around the time of Christ, said this of Hercules,

> But when they heard from him his name, his lineage and his achievements, they recommended both their country and themselves to his friendship. And Evander, […] resolved to forestall all mankind by being the first to propitiate Hercules with divine honours, and he hastily erected an improvised altar and sacrificed upon it a calf that had not known the yoke, having first communicated the oracle to Hercules and asked him to perform the initial rites.

And,

> After Hercules had settled everything in Italy according to his desire and his naval force had arrived in safety from Spain, he sacrificed to the gods the tithes of his booty and built a small town named after himself in the place where his fleet lay at anchor […]; and having gained fame and glory and received divine honours from all the inhabitants of Italy, he set sail for Sicily.[64]

A key example of deifying men can be found in the pyramids of Egypt. In studying for this book, I came across several modern accounts of the building of the great pyramid. This piqued my curiosity, and it prompted me to briefly study them. It seems to me that the modern consensus is that the Great Pyramid was built over twenty years, based on an inscription they found somewhere. There was a general agreement that they used a ramp to raise the blocks. There was an overarching contempt for

Herodotus, who had recently become one of my favorite historians. The impression I got was that he would be akin to a blogger today. In other words, he isn't reliable. Several of them said that nobody in his time (approximately 800 BC) could read the hieroglyphics. They also said that the great pyramid was built for a king before he died so that he might ascend to the stars.

The ancient accounts of Herodotus did not agree with the modern accounts. Moreover, Diodorus said, "Consequently her [Zarina] countrymen after her death, in gratitude for her benefactions and in remembrance of her virtues, built her a tomb which was far the largest of any in their land; for they erected a triangular pyramid . . ." [38] Diodorus lived around 50 BC, well after all the big pyramids were built. Herodotus wrote, "The pyramid itself was twenty years in building." [49] That's consistent. Then he wrote,

> After laying the stones for the base, they raised the remaining stones to their places by means of machines formed of short wooden planks. The first machine raised them from the ground to the top of the first step. On this there was another machine, which received the stone upon its arrival, and conveyed it to the second step, whence a third machine advanced it still higher. Either they had as many machines as there were steps in the pyramid, or possibly they had but a single machine, which, being easily moved, was transferred from tier to tier as the stone rose- both accounts are given, and therefore I mention both.

That doesn't sound like a ramp to me. He continued, "I perfectly well remember that the interpreter who read the writing to me said that the money expended in this way was 1600 talents of silver." Did he just say that someone read the inscriptions to him? Not only was he allegedly there (by his own claim), but he heard someone translate the writing on the pyramid. This is more like an investigative reporter than a blogger. One video I saw had, not one, but several experts talking about the pyramids. Either they have some powerful evidence against Herodotus, or they are all wrong about several things. The modern historians may have really good evidence. As for me, I'm not ready to call Herodotus a liar, although Diodorus did in his first book.[65] And yet Diodorus also contradicted the modern historians.

My intention here is not to build a rock solid case for how the pyramids were constructed. Instead, I want to point out that there are experts from all ages who doubt one another's testimonies. I think these historians had reason to doubt, just as they have reason to trust. You have to make up your own mind. One thing is certain, though. The writers before Christ all seem to agree that the gods were either deified men or actual gods.

Let's finish off that quote from Diodorus.

> [F]or they erected a triangular pyramid, making the length of each side three stades and the height one stade, and bringing it to a point at the top; and on the tomb they also placed a colossal gilded statue of her and accorded her the honours belonging to heroes, and all the other honours they bestowed upon her were more magnificent than those which had fallen to the lot of her ancestors.

If this is at all interesting to you, I encourage you to go back and read other descriptions Herodotus gives of Egypt, if for no other reason than to laugh at his lack of true knowledge.[66]

Let's end with two of the most important gods in the Pantheon. Diodorus wrote this of Cronus,

> Cronus, since he was the eldest of the Titans, became king and caused all men who were his subjects to change from a rude way of living to a civilized life, and visited many regions of the inhabited earth. Among all he met he introduced justice and sincerity of soul, and this is why the tradition has come down to later generations that the men of Cronus' time were good-hearted, altogether guileless, and blest with felicity. His kingdom was strongest in the western regions, where indeed he enjoyed his greatest honour; consequently, down even to comparatively recent times, among the Romans and

the Carthaginians, while their city still stood, and other neighbouring peoples, notable festivals and sacrifices were celebrated in honour of this god and many places bore his name. And because of the exceptional obedience to laws no injustice was committed by any one at any time and all the subjects of the rule of Cronus lived a life of blessedness, in the unhindered enjoyment of every pleasure. To this the poet Hesiod also bears witness in the following words:

"And they who were of Cronus' day, what time
He reigned in heav'n, lived like the gods, no care
In heart, remote and free from ills and toils
Severe, from grievous sicknesses and cares;
Old age lay not upon their limbs, but they,
Equal in strength of leg and arm, enjoyed
Endless delight of feasting far from ills,
And when death came, they sank in it as in
A sleep. And many other things were theirs:
Grain-giving earth, unploughed, bore for them fruit
Abundantly and without stint; and glad
Of heart they dwelt upon their tilth throughout
The earth, in midst of blessings manifold,
Rich in their flocks, loved by the blessed gods." [57]

Hercules did great things too. This quote is from Dionysius.

Hercules, who was the greatest commander of his age, marched at the head of a large force through all the country that lies on this side of the Ocean, destroying any despotisms that were grievous and oppressive to their subjects, or commonwealths that outraged and injured the neighbouring states, or organized bands of men who lived in the manner of savages and lawlessly put strangers to death, and in their room establishing lawful monarchies, well-ordered governments and humane and sociable modes of life. Furthermore, he mingled barbarians with Greeks, and inhabitants of the inland with dwellers on the sea coast, groups which hitherto had been distrustful and unsocial in their dealings with each other; he also built cities in desert places, turned the course of rivers that overflowed the fields, cut roads through

> inaccessible mountains, and contrived other means by which every land and sea might lie open to the use of all mankind. [...] For among the various measures of Hercules that bespoke the true general none was more worthy of admiration than his practice of carrying along with him for a time on his expeditions the prisoners taken from the captured cities, and then, after they had cheerfully assisted him in his wars, settling them in the conquered regions and bestowing on them the riches he had gained from others. It was because of these deeds that Hercules gained the greatest name and renown in Italy. [53]

As you can clearly see, both Cronus and Hercules were kings in the earth. They were celebrated while they lived, and after their deaths, venerated. This has been the rule for great kings of that time, not the exception. Inventors were remembered as well. Hades probably showed the people how to give a proper burial. Poseidon probably showed them how to be a true sailor. The last two are speculation, but surely someone figured out how to smelt iron. They were probably venerated for it. Everything that man has ever done has had inventors that turned into teachers. These people bestowed great gifts on the commoners and were remembered for it. They became immortal. Many of these people have stories that were written down, just not in my notes. You can find them and read about it, as I have done. You may just find that they are as worthy of immortality as any of us ever are.

There is a lot more to say about the gods. There are a lot of distinguishing factors for the nations. There are funny and strange things written down by these ancient geographers. Because these issues take away from the central purpose of this book, I have put these topics into my appendix. If you are interested and you believe you are likely to follow the rest of the main text to the end, I encourage you to read it now. Otherwise, we will go away from the more trusted sources to one that is doubted. If it is true, it gives us unparalleled insights into the story of early man.

Chapter 4

TRAVELS OF NOAH INTO EUROPE

I am forever indebted to Richard Lynche, who compiled his history in 1601. Not only did he give me the title for this chapter, but he gave me most of the sources for chapter three. He also got me excited about history. It's true that I was looking for a source such as his and that anyone who compiled anything like it would have sufficed, but just because anyone can write a history, doesn't mean everyone does. I found his work, and I'm grateful to him for it. (This is where you all send me a thank you note! Just kidding.) Of course, he had just as many people as I do to thank for the history he was able to compile. His history came from authors who also got the story from even earlier authors. So "thank you" to those who are dead and probably can't hear me, and "you're welcome" to those who can. We're all in the same boat. Nothing is really new with us. Nothing is new, that is, unless we made it up!

One of the sources that Lynche used to compile his information, in fact the major source, was Annio of Viterbo [67] (Annius of Viterbe, as Lynche says it). This guy was a high-ranking church official who was clearly an expert in history. His writings were not really challenged until more than fifty years after his death, at which point, he was "thoroughly discredited" by scholars. I wish I could read Latin or someone could translate some of the written works against him, because all I have of this is hearsay.

A church official writes a history, and another guy denies it. The history has implications and so does the denial. Generally, if someone says they have Berosus as a source, and they have a volume of mostly consistent text to go with their claim, I'm going to believe that they're telling me the truth and that they had the text. Being in his position in the church, he would have access to documents like it. On the other hand, if his facts are contradictory throughout, and someone accused him of making it up, it really does give us pause. Do I need to have Annio's work be credible for Lynche's work to also be? No. Lynche uses many sources that are verified. Likewise, I'm sure Annio's sources are also largely verified. We can simply go to their sources and confirm the story, which I have with Lynche for much of his.

There are some that cannot be verified though. Some of those parts are among the juiciest too. I can't even read the text of Annio either. It's not in English. What's a guy to do? I'll tell you what I'll do. I'll pass the problem off to you. I'll only add that I lean toward believing them. They have very little motivation to lie. Then I'll take you through these orchards, and you can decide if you want to pluck anything off the trees. If you want to do any more research on these two guys, I recommend getting Mike Gascoigne's book, *Forgotten History of the Western People.*[68] He has a chapter on this, and he is the main reason I ever heard of *Travels of Noah into Europe.*[69] He was kind enough to post it, and I have taken the trouble to transcribe it to text.[70] After that, I took the trouble to find someone else who transcribed it better than I did.[71]

I hope that you are willing to at least give the thing a chance, even if you don't think it is credible in the end. Some of the ideas give answers to the problems some people still have with the flood today. Even if it didn't happen the way Lynche says it did, the way he connects the dots is ingenious. He is valuable for speculation, at least.

This chapter is a summary of *Travels of Noah into Europe* (TNE) through the time of Hercules, though Lynche takes the history through to the foundation of Troy. I leave out a lot. You can imagine that massive chunks of their lives have been removed from his account too. I wonder what my life would look like through the filter of a few paragraphs. For greater detail, you will have to read TNE.

Through the text, he talks about Osyris. I have seen in other places[72] that this is a name that was given to Zeus (Jove, Jupiter, Osiris).[73] You can use all these names interchangeably. Egyptians called him Osiris, the Greeks used Zeus, the Romans used Jupiter. The best evidence that they are the same is that they are the father of Hercules.

You will need to know what it says in Genesis in order to have an understanding of the writings of Moses. If you have not read Genesis, read Chapters 1–11 now. The genealogies will be discussed later, so glance through those as well.

Another useful bit of preparation information lies in Lynche's discussion of giants. He claimed they were real. He says that Noah was one. That would make his cubit much bigger than ours, and thereby, the ark would have been larger as well. A cubit is the length of the forearm, from the elbow to the fingertips. Claims of giants would be enough for many to reject the text outright. Let us let him defend himself.

> But for so much as in this book mention is made oftentimes of strange and horrible giants, & other rare and admirable things, the reader may perhaps remain incredulous, and scarce believe them to be true, accounting them wholly fabulous, and by invention fashioned, yet to allege some authority for the confirmation thereof (leaving out infinite other examples of infallible certainty) you only shall be referred to the holy scriptures, and also unto Iosephus the Iuwish writer, who amply hath handled the apology thereof: among the rest, Nembroth, Golias, and others, are apparent, that there were Giants, and of unusual stature, strength, & proportion of body. If the authority of Boccace may be accepted, he thus writeth of himself: In my time (sayth he) there was found under the foot and hollow cavern of a mountain, not far from the city of Deprana, in the Isle of Sicilia, the body of a marvellous, huge, and strange proportioned Giant, which seemed to hold in one of his hands a mighty long piece of wood like

> unto the body of a young tree, or the mast of a ship, which so soon as it was touched, fell all into ashes and dust, but it was all garnished & wrought about with lead, which remained sound and firm, & it was found to weigh five hundred pound weight: his body also being touched, consumed, and became all powder and ashes, except certain of his bones, and three of his teeth, which were also peized, and every tooth weighed forty ounces. For the height and full stature of his body; it was conjectured by the people of that country, to be two hundred cubits long. And the same author sayeth, That his teeth were afterwards hanged up in our lady's church of Deprana, for a strange monument, and a thing of wonders and relics of memory, but leaving these matters to be further ruminated by the scrupulous, I will return to our main intendment proceeding, till I have further explained the obscurity thereof.

Two hundred cubits (approximately 300 feet or 90 meters)? This story might very well be "conjectured," but there are too many giants in the myths and history to let it go without at least a little consideration. I would also add that if we think that diversity was built into sexual reproduction, we could have all sorts of people at the beginning. [93] There have been giant human bones found.[74] It wouldn't be so surprising to us if we consider that there are genetic dwarfs and midgets now. There are entire people groups where the adult population is short.[75] Having people grow to be big shouldn't cause us excess grief. Perhaps the cubit of the little people was the measurement used for calculating the length of the giant!

He starts,

> This Noe by the descriptions of old writers was taken in those days to be a [Giant], in respect of his extraordinary nature, proportion, and [corpulence] and he was about the age (as Moses also in [the first] chapter of Genesis [affirmeth]) of five hundred years, when he begat of his wife [Tytia] (otherwise called Aretia) [these] his three first sons, {Cham, Shem, Japheth} and his [family] lived in a city called Enos, which

> was the first city in the world, and was built by Cain the son of Adam, at the foot of the mountain Libanus in the land of Syria, and in the particular province of Phoenicia, not far from the famous city of Ierusalem, situated in the holy land.

I expect that this city was pre-flood and is no longer there. You will see here, and even in Scripture, that the places that existed before the flood were said to be at post-flood locations. Jubilees (see chapter 5) and many other old documents do this. This is a difficult thing for me to accept, because the flood waters were above all the mountains. The layers of sediment all around the world are thousands of feet thick. It leads me to think that the actual locations of these places were either misidentified by Noah or by those who came shortly after him. I am willing to entertain the idea that one hill before the flood was spared from excessive sedimentation in one area of the world, but there has to be a bit more evidence than a historical speculation to cause me to accept it. I hope someone else has a good answer for this, because my little feeler is still out there trying to grasp for something.

He continues, "[O]nly the good giant Noe, among all the rest, feared God ..." He names everyone on the ark. "Titea his wife, Shem, Cham, and Iaphet, their children, and Pandora, Noela, & Noegla, their wives ..." Then came the flood. The flood was not local. It wiped out all animals with breath on the face of the earth.

> Noe then seeing himself thus left the sole King, Monarch, Emperor, Patriarch, Lord and Master of the whole universal land, remained wondrously astonished at this so strange and sense amazing accident: and passing along the land, he found on a plain a fair pillar of marble, whereon he carefully engraved and set down the deluge and general inundation of the world in the form of an historical discourse: & this stone (as it is reported) is called at this day by the inhabitants thereabouts, Myri-Adam, which interpreted, signifies the issue of Noe, and it standeth in the county of Armenia ...

There are several things to comment on here. Noah was king. He made a monument to remember the flood. He wrote down what happened! If Noah could write, and he's only two living people removed from Adam (Adam, Enoch, Noah), there is not really any such thing as prehistoric. It is also noteworthy that he lived in Armenia, which is south of the Black Sea. Berosus was a Chaldean, which is just south of the Black Sea. He was in a place where learning would have grown and flourished early on. Their history might have been exceptional because of it. Berosus would have been in a better position to write down the deeds of Noah than any other Greek of his day. This is all speculation, but you can keep it in mind as we go on.

> Noe thus living in Armenia, instructed these his children in the knowledge of sacred Theology, and in rites belonging to religion and holy sacrifices, as also in the understanding of human manners and secrecies of Nature, of which he himself had composed many books, which afterward the priests and churchmen of Scythia and Armenia, preserved and kept in great regard and reverence.

Noah was a religious man, and he taught his children how to sacrifice. He wrote books. Next, Lynche writes down the other sons of Noah.

> It is written, That Noe begat of his wife Tytea after the flood, thirty children, viz. Tuyscon the Great, Prometheus, Iapetus, Macrus, and the sixteen Titans which were all Giants: also Cranus, Granaus, Oceanus, and Tipheus; and of daughters, Araxa surnamed the Great, Regina, Pandora, Cranua, and Thetis: some authors do allege more, but for brevity's sake we will not further contend with others opinions.

The Scythians have a name for him. "For this cause he was called among the Scythians, Ogyges Saga, which interpreted from the Scythian language, signifies as much as Great Patriarch, sovereign Priest, and mighty Sacrificer." The Scythians lived just north of the Black Sea. This would be another unique perspective that Berosus brings to the table. It makes the fabrication of Annio seem a bit less fabricated. The details are fitting together nicely.

Lynche then mentions Ham. "Cham was the least in his father's favour, who also by reason of his Magic art (wherein he had great knowledge) was called Zoroast…" He wrote of a curse he cast on his father while he was drunk, so he couldn't make use of women. With thirty kids, a curse like this doesn't seem very likely. I'm not pretending that these details are certain. This one seems a bit shady to me.

"Noe, surnamed Ianus, began to exhort the princes and chiefs of this family…" I mention this because we see later that the first month of the year was named for him. Janus shows up in mythology too.

I have mentioned that the land was divided in three. (See page 45, 90, 114 & 143) I have read this fact in numerous places, and I'm sad to say, I didn't write them all down. I only got a few. The land was divided as follows: "To Sem, surnamed Melchisedech, he appointed Asia…" "He afterwards built the city of Salem, now called Ierusalem, and he lived even until the time of Abraham." "Unto Iaphet his brother was allotted Europe…" Cham got the rest, which is Africa. Annius says "Philo the Iew" confirms this. In the book of Jubilees, it says they casted lots for the division and that Noah was particularly happy for Shem. It said that Eden was in that section.[76] I think it's also useful to point to the fact that Sem was called Melchisedech. Jasher and Hebrews say that he was the king of Salem. Salem was later called Jerusalem.[77] Now that's an old city! Genesis says that in the days of Peleg, the land was divided. I read in several places that this was the event they were referring to.

So what did Noah do while he lived three hundred years after the flood, being king of the whole world? He sailed. He went from nation to nation, depositing people, plants, and animals.

> [I]nto which country of Italy Noe also afterward arrived and left behind him certain of his people…
>
> That as he passed through all those countries, he always left people behind him to inhabit and increase in those countries, distributing unto every number certain quarters to remain in: and after this time, in short space many countries were again re-inhabited and peopled afresh, which since the flood were desolate, and lay naked and depopulat.
>
> Noe began to divide kingdoms, & also to erect monarchies in the world: of which, Nembroth the Giant, the son of this nephew Cus, who was the son of Cham, was first of all established…

Nembroth is Nimrod according to Genesis 10:8 and Josephus. Noah was inclined toward certain locations more than others.

> Noe divided four particular kingdoms in Europe, viz. the kingdom of Italy, Spain, France and Almaigne: for in Italy reigned Comerus Gallus, the eldest son of Iaphet: in Spain ruled Tuball (called also Iuball) the fifteenth son of Iaphet: in France Samothes (surnamed Dis) Iaphet's fourth son: and over Almaign, (now called Germany) governed the Giant Tuyscon, one of the sons of Noe.

All these claims are verified in many places. A quick and easy book to show a map of the descendants of Noah is *Noah's Three Sons* by Arthur Custance. [39] You can also see the map at the end of this book to see where they all went.

> These things at home thus established, Noe (surnamed Ianus) with his wife Titea, and many multitudes of people besides, began his voyage (which was eight score and nine years after the flood, and in the eight and thirtieth year of the reign of Nembroth) toward Hyrcania, which he then peopled, and called them after his own name Ianij.

He went other places after that.

The idea that Noah went from place to place, setting up nations and depositing people, is a powerful argument with regard to biogeography. I'm not saying that Noah planted the Australian Aborigines with kangaroos, and the Pacific Islanders certainly populated late in comparison to the Europeans, but the principal is the same. The world was set up. It was populated in spores, not necessarily in waves. Again, this is speculation. It helps that this was written in a time before people doubted the Bible. Lynche didn't make it up as an answer to my question.

I find the next quote very interesting. Lynche is treating this text as history. He's in no doubt that what happened, happened.

> Now it is not written, whether he went this journey into Italy by land or sea, notwithstanding: it is likely, and agreeth with good probability that in this his voyage he would not pass by without visiting the wise prince, his nephew Samothes, the brother of Tuball king of Spain, who was by his appointment created the first king of France, as is before touched, and he had reigned about this time six score years, and lived after this in peace and tranquillity five and thirty years and upward.

He then begins in on Ham's evil deeds. Italy was taken over by Ham's progeny and tormented by tyrants. Ianus (or Noah, giver of wine) drove them out and set up a good government. He founded many cities, two of which later became the Vatican and Viterbe. He wrote this stuff down in books. This part lends to the idea that the story was made up, or at best, hopeful. When you find that the city you live in was among the earliest and set up by Noah himself, it's playing to one's own pride. Conversely, if the account was true, perhaps that's why Annio chose to live in Viterbo and change his name to something historic. The guy was obsessed with history.

Having such an ancient city would also lend to the establishment of a very ancient historical archive. You can decide what you want to believe about this, but don't cast judgment on the text just yet. "Sabatius Saga, surnamed Saturn" was driven out of Armenia by Nimrod's son, Iupiter Belus. He fled to Italy, and Noah made him king over the Aborigines, whom he banished from Italy to Sicilia. These Aborigines are written about in all sorts of histories. I didn't write it down, but you have my sources. You can easily find them.

"Titea the great, Noe's wife, began in those times first to set up the order of Nuns, and ceremonies of Vestal virgins ..." "Saturne likewise very painfully instructed to the people in the tillage, and in the nature of soils ..." Poor old man, using his plow ...

> Noe Ianus finding & perceiving his end to approach, and that now his lustiness and vigour of spirits began to shrink and decrease, created one of his sons, called Cranus, the King and Patriarch over the Iangenes (which are now called Tuscanes) and the sixth year after departed this life ..."

Cranus (one of the Titans) was given dominion over Tuscanes (Italy) before Noah died. This is enough to make a guy cry: Noah died 346 years after the flood, 480 years before the foundation of Troy, and 1967 BC, when he was 950. Remember that Noah lived a long time. Many of his grandchildren were dead before he was, and they lived a long time.

> The death of this good King and Patriarch possessed almost all the people in the world with great sorrow and lamentation, and especially the Armenians and Italians, who in most honourable manner celebrated his obsequies with such their then used rites and ceremonies, and afterward dedicated and attributed unto him divine honours and godlike adorations, building and consecrating temples and holy altars unto him, calling him by diverse and several names and titles, as the Sun, the Heaven, the Seed of the world, the Father of the gods, the Soul of the world, the God of peace, the giver of justice and holiness, the expulser of things hurtful: also their children and successors called him Ianus, Geniius,

> Quadrifons, [Enotrius], Ogyges, Vertumnus, Vadymon, Protheus, Multisors, Diespiter, and Iupiter…
>
> In honour of him also at this day the first month of the year is called after his own name Ianuarius, as Servius in his Aneidas affirmeth.

Think of Noah next time January rolls around. He was an honorable man.

He touches on the mood of the day: "[I]n those days all those princes, rulers, and governors that had lived virtuously, justly, and godly, and have commanded their people with [mildness], equity, and uprightness, were entermed gods…" And Noah's wife "Titea his wife held in great reverence, worship, and holy esteem, who was called also Vesta, Aretia, Terra, Regina sacrorum, magna Cybeles, Materque deorum, atque Vestalium Princeps, sive Abbatißa, as Berosus and other writers affirm."

With Noah gone, he starts recounting the history of Ham (Cham or Pan,[78] founder of Egypt).

> [I]t shall not be now impertinent something to remember and speak of the wicked and abominable life of his son Cham, which although of itself it be worthless of any recapitulation or recital, yet to descend to the line all genealogy of the Lybian Hercules the Great, it cannot be well omitted: from which Hercules, Dardanus the first founder and erector of Troy, descended and came.

Ham was so evil that Lynche didn't even want to talk about him. Ham was the grandfather of Hercules, whose descendants founded Troy. It might be useful to note here that we have discovered Troy.[79] Someone took the mythology seriously and proved what was doubted by so many at the time: that Troy was real. The story was quite interesting, but I'll leave you to find it. "It is written, that Cham had one sister which was called Rhea, married to Hammon, king of Lybia, who also was enamoured of one other fair woman, called Almanthea, and had of her by adulterous means, a son, whose name afterwards was Dionysus…"

I want you to notice that it was written. This isn't speculated or made up; at least it isn't by Lynche.

Diodorus tells this same story when recounting the history as told by the Atlantians (see my appendix). It's also interesting that Dionysus was a direct son of Ham. Rhea left her husband for Ham. "Rhea had a son of her husband Cham, called Osyris …" Dionysus took care of his little brother. "Notwithstanding, he [Dionysus] used Osyris (the young son of Cham and Rhea) with great clemency and mercy, and received him as his adopted child, and in remembrance of his father called him also Hammon …" Osiris[80] was later to be a famous man, but even emperors have childhood heroes. "[O]ver whom he appointed as schoolmaster and tutor, a learned man called Olympus, of whom afterwards Osyris took his name, and was surnamed Olympicus."

The inbreeding gets even better, as Rhea and Ham have a daughter that will marry their son. "Rhea was presently upon this, delivered of a daughter called Iuno, which was also called Isis the Great …" Juno and Isis are very famous names in mythology. Notice that they are the same person. Ham took an army to battle with Nimrod, and Nimrod won. Ham was slain in the battle, thus ended the infamous Ham.

Lynche was occupied in his work by three people we're interested in. We have already addressed the deeds of Noah. The second was the grandson of Noah through Ham, Osiris. "Osyris before spoken of (the adopted son of Dionysus, king of Lybia) and Isis his sister …" married. They were sixty and fifty, respectively, but "[O]ur author Berosus terms them very youthful …" Again, it is interesting to see how he doesn't even question the validity of the text he uses. He's convinced that the stories in each of the histories match up. In all honesty, I don't see many contradictions myself. Either the forger was really careful, or we have the genuine article. Again, I let you decide.

Osiris went around the world, teaching farming and other skills, and he gained a really good reputation. "The chief place of command in all his [Osyris] army, he appointed unto his eldest son Hercules of Lybia, who upon his escutcheon and arms, bare depainted the shape of a crowned Lion rampant, holding in his forefeet a mighty hatchet."

He then chases a rabbit for a little while, but it is useful information to anyone studying this time in history. "And in those times all good and just princes were called gods, as Pan, Apollo, Iupiter, and infinite others, with their goddesses, muses, and nymphs." Of course, we already touched on this when recounting the histories in chapter three.

"This mighty, powerful, and gallant army thus gathered together, the Emperor Osyris proceedeth in his intended voyage ..." to Africa, India, and Ethiopia, teaching them as he went. It is interesting to me that he went to India. These guys were not averse to travel.

> From thence he passed into another province called Emathia, in which also ruled many bloody cruel Giants, all which he clean extirpated, destroyed, and subdued, settling the country in peaceable quietness and security, over which he appointed to be commander, one of his own sons before spoken of, called Macedon, who afterwards called the country after his own name, Macedonia, and the people Macedonians ..."

So we meet the giants. They are almost always cruel, but we do see kind giants from time to time in these accounts. I wonder if they were cruel by nature or if they developed that way. If a kid is bigger than all his other friends, he would be able to take what he wanted. That would carry over into adulthood. Who would befriend a man who would crush them to get his way? Who would marry him?

Osiris went to many countries, but he's famous in Italy. "The country of Italy about this time was extremely oppressed with the tyranny & and bloody fashions of infinite numbers of Giants that thereabouts then lived called Titans ..." He slew many of these giants. "Osyris [...] given many titles & and names [...] as Iupiter Iustus, Dux, Rex, Consultor, Cuius regnum perpetuum est, & habitalio in Olympo ..." Zeus was the originator of justice (Iupieter Iustus). Typhon, a giant, murdered Osiris. Isis held a funeral for Osiris, who died two hundred years too early at three hundred years old. She also got her sons to revenge on Typhon. She was then empress in his place. This is confirmed by Diodorus.[81]

Let's take a minute to consider what was said at the beginning of chapter three. Most historians wrote down their local traditions. A man that lived three hundred years will outlast the historian who is making the biography, and the end of the life of the man would not be in the full account of his deeds unless that same biographer is still writing, or a later historian is able to connect the dots. Any monuments or stories handed down by word of mouth would be flawed in that they didn't have the end of the story. To the locals, maybe Zeus went on a journey, and when he never came back, they assumed that he went to Olympus to set up his throne. We have only to speculate why Hercules didn't have the official account laid out for us. Perhaps Hercules wasn't much of an intellectual. He was an adventurer and a philanderer. He was more interested in physical posterity than he was in historical posterity. We can only guess.

Now we move on to Hercules. Hercules wandered, killed giants, and named Libya after himself. Read the text for more details. Hercules, who liberated Spain, appointed his son as king.

> Hispalus was crowned and invested in the kingdom of Spain by his father Hercules, in the six and thirtieth year of Baleus (the second of that name) the eleventh king of Babylon [1727 BC] for Hercules was born presently after the death of Ninus, the third king of Babylon, from whose death unto the six and thirtieth year of Baleus, the eleventh king, were just two hundred fourscore and ten years: so that by this means it may clearly be perceived, in what time and what age this Lybian Hercules so arrived in Gaul, being presently after the coronation of his son Hispalus in Spain.[82]

Ninus was Nimrod.

> From thence he descended and came into Italy, where he fully revenged himself of those inhumane and lawless Giants, which were the death of his own father Iupiter Iustus [Osyris]: and after all tumults quieted, and the resistants subdued, he fell to peaceable laws to the people and to instruct them very carefully in matters of civil association & orderly living...

It's as though Lynche remembered something he forgot to say about Noah, and he comes briefly back to his story. "After this his return into Armenia, having there rested himself some one and twenty years, he began to invent the foundations of great cities..." He put Nimrod over Babylon first. "[Noah] instituted and established for the king of the Gauls one of his kinsmen called Samothes, surnamed Dis, the fourth son of Iaphet [Javan?], a man very wise and well governed." (2093 BC) He mentions in there that Saturn was not a person's name, but a title. Jupiter is also a title.[83]

Hercules reigned in Italy for twenty years (that's the same as Noah and Osyris) and did lots of stuff there, including building, astronomy, and botany.

> Hercules in that country, now very aged [...] had now given over the desire of rule and principality, and gloried in [...] his own [...] labours [...] for indeed he was the Monarch and prince almost of all the world, [...] not by oppressions, tyranny, or unlawfulness, but by the subduing of wicked and ungodly giants, the disposing of all usurpers and bloody governors, & by the abolishing and rooting out of all devilish and inhumane customs then observed in those days among the poor and faith-wanting vulgars in those times of error. In these his times of privateness and retired living which he spent in Spain, he builded and caused to be erected many great towns, cities, and villages; for which cause the people of that country still call him Hercules the builder. Besides this,

> also he gave and addicted himself to the finding out of the natures of strange herbs, and to the study of Astronomy, and to the Magic art, wherein he wondrous deeply was seen, and excellently well read; but he never applied the use thereof but unto the good and general commodity of the country.

He addresses in some detail the difference between the three Herculeses of history—the first being the most magnificent. Hercules of Libya was called by many other names.

> [Hercules] was called also by these names, as Her, Hercol, Arno, Musarno: and they thus signify and are englished from the Hebrew tongue, as S. Ierome and others expound it: Her signifieth hair, Hercol all covered over with hair, Arno signifieth a Lion, and Musarno the portraiture of effigies of a Lion, and these names were thus ascribed unto him, for that he always wore for his upper garment the hair skins of Lions, Bears, Leopards, and other such beasts, and for that on his shield or target was depainted and drawn the shape and form of a Lion...

Only a man could be called "hair." They celebrated him.

> [T]he people of Spain erected many most sumptuous and costly monuments, and bestowed upon him [Hercules] a wonderful, rich and stately tomb, which as some hold, was built hard by that place, which as we now call them, the Gades, pillars, or columns of Hercules are seated upon, being not far from the famous straights of Gibraltar.

It is useful to point out here that this monument was well-known during that time. They called it the Strait of Hercules (which is between Morocco and Spain) and the Pillars of Hercules, most frequently. "[T]he kingdom of Spain next after Hercules, succeeded Hesperus, being the twelfth king and governor thereof, & who was brother unto the renowned Atlas..."

Then we move to France.

> [F]irst concerning the people of France, they were first of all called Samothei, of Samothes their king, then Celti, then Galatij, after that Belgae, of their king and Patriarch Beligius, after that Galli, and since that Francigenae or Franci. The names in like manner of the people of Germany varied and differed very often and severally: For the first name that ever that people received, were Tuyscones, of Tuyscon one of Noes sons, the first that ever was king and ruler over that country. After that they were called Gambrivij, then Ingheones, after that, Ifteones, Suevi, and Vandali, then also Thetanes, Theutontes, Vindelici, Vandalici, after that Alemanni, and last of all, of the Romans (as some hold) they were generally entearmed Germani. So that by these it is plainly shown, how almost all countries and nations have at diverse times been diversely and differingly called…

I think this speaks for itself. Lynche says it, but it's easily verified. Nations were named, and those names were tainted through the generations.

Let's talk about Atlas for a little while. "Hesperus had not there long reigned, but he was expulsed and driven out of his country by violent and oppressive means by his brother Atlas the giant, surnamed Italus…" He wasn't as nice as we would like him to be.

> Atlas Italus, not contented sufficiently with the principality and dominion of Spain (as overambitiously thoughted) came also into Italy, and overswayed by his mightiness and power all the country round about, and called all the country generally after his own name, Italia…

Italy was named for Atlas.

> This Italus Atlas by his descent was of the linage of Iaphet, and of his son Comerus Gallus, the first king of Italy; and it was he which according to the opinions of many, excelled most of all men then living, in the knowledge of Astrology,

for which cause, the [busy] Poets feigned, that he supported and upheld the heavens with his shoulders.

It is probably helpful to say here that I have read names that were associated with scores of countries, regions, and landmarks. I have more to say about Atlas being the first to call the country *Italy* (Read in the section on Eusebius, page 125). We can say with certainty that the "atlas" that you have on your bookshelf was named for him, and so was Atlantis. The Atlantic Ocean was too! The guy was famous enough to survive to our time. That's impressive enough; Italy is icing on the cake.

Galatheus,

> [O]f him and of his name the country generally was called Gaul, and so continued, and the people thereof termed Gaulons, which by corruption and overturning of many ages and times, are now in some part of the country called Wallons, and which before Galatheus, were called Samothei or Celti.

I throw this one in to show that Noah wasn't the only one that lived a long time. Many people of that time did.

> This their goddess Isis, otherwise called by the names of Cares, Iuno, Frugifera, Legifera, and others, was by all probability and by the opinion of all writers a woman of wonderful long life and many years, for at her now arrival and coming to this marriage into Italy, she was at least four hundred and fifty years old, as she that was born in the first year of the reign of Semiramis queen of Babylon, and lived in the whole at the least six hundred and sixteen years, for she was living after the first destruction and desolation of Troy, by the space of forty years or near thereabouts, as almost all writers have delivered in their opinions to the same purpose and effect.

She was a teacher. She lived a long time, and she probably learned a few things along the way. "[A]nd that she had travelled almost all these parts of Europe, instructing and teaching the poor ignorant people the use of many things then unknown & unfound out."

> And thus it hath been with great care and diligence laboured to find out the truest Historians for the deriving of Dardanus, and consequently this king Priamus, from the race and line of the first prince and Patriarch, Noe, with the particular succession of kings and emperors of Europe, as hath been warranted by the authorities and writings of very learned and authentic authors.

He says he took from the truest historians. If we can't trust those histories, whose can we trust? Who can argue that they were learned? Read the source materials yourself if you are in doubt about their understanding of history.

So that's it. That is what I wanted to pick from Lynche, and you can throw it all out if you want to. He said much more than I wrote down, and if you read the text carefully, you can glean so much more than my comments discovered. Some of what he said is contradicted elsewhere, but it happens seldom enough that we might just as well wonder if the other source is flawed. One thing is certain: Lynche didn't make it up. If there was a forgery, it was much older than him. I quoted many sources in chapter three that verify not only the general feeling about the history but many of the particulars as well. If the forgery was started by Annio in the fifteenth century, it was only the lesser details that he made up, not the story as a whole. If he was a fraud, it does not take much away from my conclusion. If he was not a fraud, his insights are remarkable. Many of the accounts I read about Annio said that he genuinely believed his sources to be true. We have a choice. We either think that these guys were pulling from genuine sources and making up stories around them, or we believe they use entirely genuine sources, as I have tried to do, and commented on them. Maybe he was right. Maybe he was duped. Both choices have their implications. Either way, we still have to make an account for the even more impressive mountain of evidence that is to follow in the sources that the religious have always found to be accurate for the purposes of history.

Chapter 5

RELIGIOUS TEXTS

There is an overwhelming bias in the area of science, and I think it has spilled over into history too, that religious people and their perspectives are not reliable. They are not reliable because some of their beliefs are based in things that are not tangible. If that's your position, I'm very much surprised that you got this far into my book. If you hold this position, you are a fool. I don't say that because I have read it in religious texts. I say that because it seems right to me. If you believe a thing cannot exist without being seen, you are a fool. Abstract thought, such as the fact that you are a fool, exists.

Don't take my harsh words the wrong way. People can change. A wise man can become a fool. Likewise, a fool can become wise. How do I know this? I've seen it happen. It's observable! How would I recommend you change? How do you gain wisdom?

Think about this. Everywhere across the globe, there are things happening. There are so many things happening that you can't possibly keep track of more than just a sliver of the events that are going on. Every person, not ten, or a thousand, but billions of people are crafting their futures every minute. We can't possibly keep track of all these independent minds. Beyond those, there are animals of all sorts, every one of which is out to make a life for itself. Every one of these creatures is able to make choices. They plan, or design, their futures. A river cannot. A tornado doesn't care. What is it that makes us capable of planning? There is something unique about life. If the law of causation (or the law of cause and effect) holds true, we cannot have life without other life to give it. Ultimately, something outside of scientific law had to start this ball rolling. That something might be invisible.

We build all sorts of machines to test for things we cannot see. Our vision is limited, to say the least. Much of what we could see is hidden in plain sight, and yet many refuse to see it. What is it about supernatural events that makes people rigid with indignity? What about the unseen is so offensive? I could come up with hundreds of times in my life where I thought something was impossible, and yet someone did it, or something couldn't exist, and later I found that it did. There were many times in my life where I was foolish and arrogant. I was humbled.

Evidence of design is everywhere. Even this book was written with a purpose. If you put this book down and you think about design, even with your eyes shut, you will be subject to conclusions stemming from your own design. If you wander into a clearing in a forest, and you see a little pile of rocks in the dead center of the clearing, you know with certainty that the pile of rocks was the product of design. Your mind would immediately jump to, "I wonder who put this here." Then to, "I wonder why?" A virus is far more impressive than a pile of rocks. Our bodies are even more profound. Happenstance could never engineer such a fine machine as we have in our bodies any more than a field could engineer a pile of rocks. Don't deceive yourself. If you found the pile in the middle of a valley on Mars, you would assume that life put it there. You know as well as anyone that we're here for a purpose. If you don't see that, it is because you have chosen to be ignorant. Open your eyes. Become wise. If you do not pick this path, you will not see truth in my conclusions. It will not be at all because you are smarter than I am (which is possible) or that you're not as gullible as I am, but it will be because you have chosen to be stupid. I cannot help you.

Religious historians, or historians who do not have a problem accepting that there may have been an invisible cause, have accurately compiled histories as well. They tell of the mistakes of mankind and the response of God. We will deal with three of these documents: Genesis, Jubilees, and Jasher. Genesis was written by Moses, though some think he compiled and edited it as opposed to pulling it out of the air. Jubilees was presumably written by a Pharisee a couple hundred years BC. It was highly regarded by the Ethiopian church.[84] Jasher was written before Samuel or Joshua, as both books point to it.[85] The age and authorship of the text is not sure, but they had a manuscript in the thirteenth century in Spain, written in ancient Hebrew. Some think that it was made up at this point, but others hold the text to be the actual book of Jasher, removed from Jerusalem with the Jews, who were taken captive to Spain.[86] I have read the text, and if it is a forgery, it is a very good one. You can decide for yourself just how much credit you want to give to it.

I'll talk more about extra-canonical books at the end of this section. In the next chapter, we will quote religious Jews and Christians from millennia ago to see what they have to say about early man.

Genesis

There is a lot to be said about Genesis. The exact origin of the book is uncertain, but you have to remember that uncertainty doesn't equate to falsity. There are commentators throughout history that have written volumes of information about Genesis, and I am certain that if I even tried to give any more than a simple exposition, I'd be wasting your time. So many others do this better than I could. First, read the text. If you don't have time for that, read at least the first ten or so chapters.

He doesn't start with the sun. God creates light first. I quoted Philo earlier, who makes this point. There was evening and morning without the sun.

There is a lot of speculation regarding what the firmament might have been. What it means is "expanded surface." It is the word used to describe where birds fly. But he's separating firmaments. You could see it as water below the earth from the water above it. You can see it as water in the clouds, apart from the water in the seas. You could see it as a canopy above the earth, either ice or water. Any of the three would fit the text. They are all speculation.

Notice that plants were created on the third day. It is true that the Hebrew word for day *can* mean an inexact period of time (some day), but the people who want to make it anything other than a day have to account for the plants living without the sun, which was made the next day. If they are able to attribute the thing to miracle, I say it's better to go with the miracle that is the plain reading of the text. When the day is spoken of with specificity (such as we would say, "day one of the trial"), there's no real good reason or precedent for changing the meaning. In fact, every place *day* is used with a number in Genesis after the Creation account, it always means a normal day. There's no good reason to think this principle should change for the enumerated days of Genesis 1. As if that wasn't enough, the author specifies that there was evening and morning. It was only one cycle.

The stars were made on day four. This is a problem for someone who sees a large universe. How does the light from stars that are billions of light-years away get to us within the space of a couple thousand years? Why do we see supernovas happening now, when it is presumed that they are a result of thermodynamics and decay? I don't have all the answers to these questions, but I do know we can slow down light.[87] If we can slow it down, it seems possible to speed it up. We should take some things on faith.

I'll also mention here that there are features on the moon and other areas in our solar system that lend support to Walt Brown's hydroplate theory. [24] If the waters from below the earth, under heat and pressure, broke out, we would see very heavy rain. We might find water on the moon.[88] We actually see a lot more damage to the front side of the moon (the side that faces earth) than we do the back side. There are lava flows and very large craters. Comets would be shot out into an oblong orbit of our sun. Maybe some of the asteroids past Mars have something to do with it. Mars has evidence of massive water flows. If you find this topic interesting, read his book.

God made birds and fish on the fifth day. Then He made all the land animals on the sixth. Evolutionists often make the point that there is similarity between creatures. If God is anything like His people, which is implied by the phrase, "We are made in his image," wouldn't it make sense to make a creature, then take some of the themes from that creature to make another one? That's what I would do. If we have sections of DNA that resemble other animals, it is not inconsistent with Genesis.

The text says that plants were given for food. Many speculate that there were no animals eaten before the flood. There was also no death in Eden. Some people complain that this would mean that there was no digestion, because microbes are integral to that process. The distinction for life here was with the breath that came from God. If you have a nose and it breathes, you are alive in the biblical sense. This breath of God is important when we get to the flood as well. Noah took all that had the breath of God onto the ark.

Let me mention here that there are many references to extinct creatures in the Bible. Read Job 40 and 41, and see if you think a hippo's tail sways like a cedar tree or that a crocodile can't be stabbed with a spear. Search for unicorn and dragon in a King James Version Bible search tool. Whether these were actual dragons or unicorns, as are described in the legends of England and elsewhere, you can research for yourself. There are more examples of these kinds of animals all over in history. Griffins might have been protoceratops. There are animal lists all through history where they talk about dragons as though they are real.[89] People describe encounters with them in detail. Read *Beowulf*.[90] There might be many animals that we have descriptions of that we have not found fossils for. A single paragraph does not do this topic justice, but that's all I have the space for. There are a lot of other people who have taken this topic on. I will leave it with two subjects. One is the human with dinosaur footprints found in Glen Rose, Texas. If you doubt the reliability of these prints, watch this video featuring Willie E. Dye, called Divine Design.[91] The other is the Ica stones. Read Dennis Swift's book for information about that. [92] There are pottery pieces exhumed in Peru that show dinosaurs living with man. Of course, both of these issues are supposed to be false data, if the evolutionists are to be believed. I only advise that you look at the data before you make up your mind. Of course, someone who is committed to an old earth has to deny these kinds of evidence.

Then we come to the flood. There are many books written on this topic, and I don't advise reading any one over the other. I will only take you through a couple of arguments to help you get the broad categories in place. As I said, only the animals with the breath of life were taken onto the ark. This was more than likely a divine coordination, as Jasher (6:2) says that the animals came to Noah. There's a major difference between a young bird or an egg and an ostrich. You wouldn't have to take on a full grown giant tortoise. The youthful animals take less room, and will produce more offspring after they get off the boat. Diversity back then was greater than it is now. This is confirmed by breeding. Every generation loses its genetic material and needs to have someone from a distant line to come and put what was lost back into their kids. [93] Blood types are a good example of this. You can have type A, B, AB, or O. You can't get any one type without both of your parents. The water in the ocean was fresh at the start, with pockets of salt water. Rivers and vents have continually added salt and other minerals to the water, giving it what it has now.

The ark was tossed around during the flood, as Jasher says (6:27–31). Noah asked God for peace. Some plants were probably deposited on the newly exposed land, having floated on trees or by their own buoyancy. The ocean was likely to be warm, making any part of the world habitable at the coast. It would produce great evaporation, even with cold air. We would expect lots of airborne dust and water vapor to block out the sunlight, creating cold air and snow. These are perfect conditions for an ice age.[94] If you're in doubt as to how fast land that comes out of water can allow for life, look at Krakatoa and Surtsey, Iceland. [17] It doesn't take long. The waters took a while to recede. Look for images of the continental shelf. Most of the land was connected. If the ocean level was lower, due to more ice on the caps and water on the land, you could walk to the Americas from Russia or to Australia from China. In fact, there are many evidences throughout the Mediterranean and elsewhere that show the buildings of man were built under the ocean. Either that or the ocean was raised. (You might think that the land sank. This would be reasonable in one location but not in as many as there are. Search for sunken cities.) Yonaguni is a spectacular example of this. [95]

The ark landed, and the waters receded. Noah bore children, they bore grandchildren. As with the line from Adam to Noah, you have to see a chart in order to grasp this fact. The fathers lived to see many generations. Noah lived three hundred years after the flood, and Abraham was around at the same time as Noah. Shem lived even longer than that after the flood. Simple arithmetic shows that the population could grow fast when people were living a long time and having lots of kids. God commanded that they be fruitful. You could easily have millions by the time of Abraham.

There is so much more than I wrote here. I barely even scratched the surface. If there was one document I think you should look into when looking for information about early man, Genesis is it. Find books and commentaries about it, especially some of the church fathers' or early Jewish commentaries. They didn't have as strong an influence from the uniformitarians as we have today. You might find that they're a little less biased than their modern counterparts.

The Book of Jubilees

This is the book that is likely to be the youngest of any of the three books we treat here. From the introduction, "The Book of Jubilees was written in Hebrew by a Pharisee between the year of the accession of Hyrcanus to the high priesthood in and his breach with the Pharisees some years before his death in 105 BC." [84] I have found that many groups of people revere it. If it is God's perspective that we not revere it as scripture, it can at least be useful as history, and this is the position I take on the text. The person who wrote it knew a lot about the Jewish perspective on origins and especially, as the book's title would indicate, Jewish festivals. It says that the book was given to Moses on Sinai, and that an "angel of the presence" delivered the message (Prologue, Jub. 1:27).

This section is a summary of the text of Jubilees through the time of Noah and Shem. It starts with the animals of creation. I have heard many people scoff at the talking snake of Eden. Well, as ironic as it seems, it might help to know that all the animals talked at that point.

> And on that day [Adam's removal from the garden] was closed the mouth of all beasts, and of cattle, and of birds, and of whatever walks, and of whatever moves, so that they could no longer speak: for they had all spoken one with another with one lip and with one tongue.

It has been shown over and over through history that the first man born to Adam had to have his sister as a wife. Otherwise, God would have to make more people. Well, we can be confident in the fact that we all are products of incest. "And Cain took Awan his sister to be his wife and she bare him Enoch at the close of the fourth jubilee." And it happens again. "Enos took Noam his sister to be his wife ..." There are many others like this in this part of Jubilees.

Like many others after him, Enoch discovered writing. Adam was still around when Enoch lived, so "prehistory" is entirely in the minds of the historians.

> [H]e called his name Enoch. And he was the first among men that are born on earth who learnt writing and knowledge and wisdom and who wrote down the signs of heaven according to the order of their months in a book, that men might know the seasons of the years according to the order of their separate months. And he was the first to write a testimony and he testified to the sons of men among the gen-

> erations of the earth, and recounted the weeks of the jubilees, and made known to them the days of the years, and set in order the months and recounted the Sabbaths of the years as we made (them), known to him.

Then we come back to Noah.

> And in the twenty-fifth [1205 AM] jubilee Noah took to himself a wife, and her name was Emzara, the daughter of Rake'el, the daughter of his father's brother, in the first year in the fifth week [1207 AM]: and in the third year thereof she bare him Shem, in the fifth year thereof [1209 AM] she bare him Ham, and in the first year in the sixth week [1212 AM] she bare him Japheth.

Obviously someone inserted these dates into the text, but I find them useful. AM is anno mundi, or since the Creation.

Then the author makes some powerful statements about God and his character. Why would He have used the flood to destroy the earth? What a heartless thing for a loving God to do, eh?

> In regard to all He will judge, the great according to his greatness, and the small according to his smallness, and each according to his way. And He is not one who will regard the person (of any), nor is He one who will receive gifts, if He says that He will execute judgment on each: if one gave everything that is on the earth, He will not regard the gifts or the person (of any), nor accept anything at his hands, for He is a righteous judge. [And of the children of Israel it has been written and ordained: If they turn to him in righteousness He will forgive all their transgressions and pardon all their sins.

Turn to God. Do good, and he will take away our sins.[96] Okay, let's do it! Noah taught:

> For owing to these three things came the flood upon the earth, namely, owing to the fornication wherein the Watchers against the law of their ordinances went a whoring after the daughters of men, and took themselves wives of all which they chose: and they made the beginning of uncleanness. And they begat sons the Naphidim, and they were all unlike, and they devoured one another: and the Giants slew the Naphil, and the Naphil slew the Eljo, and the Eljo mankind, and one man another. And every one sold himself to work iniquity and to shed much blood, and the earth was filled with iniquity. And after this they sinned against the beasts and birds, and all that moves and walks on the earth: and much blood was shed on the earth, and every imagination and desire of men imagined vanity and evil continually. And the Lord destroyed everything from off the face of the earth; because of the wickedness of their deeds, and because of the blood which they had shed in the midst of the earth...

Many people wonder what was divided in the days of Peleg. I have read this in many places, and I'm convinced that the continents were divided between Noah's three sons.

> [S]he bare him son, and he called his name Peleg; for in the days when he was born the children of Noah began to divide the earth amongst themselves: for this reason he called his name Peleg. And they divided (it) secretly amongst themselves, and told it to Noah. And it came to pass in the beginning of the thirty-third jubilee [1569 AM] that they divided the earth into three parts, for Shem and Ham and Japheth, according to the inheritance of each, in the first year in the first week, when one of us who had been sent, was with them. And he called his sons, and they drew nigh to him, they and their children, and he divided the earth into the lots, which his three sons were to take in possession, and they reached forth their hands, and took the writing out of the bosom of Noah, their father.

They cast lots for land, which is described in too much detail to repeat it here. It also mentions several times that Eden was not covered up by sediment. It then goes through each of the grandsons of Noah and which lands they were allotted.

> And thus the sons of Noah divided unto their sons in the presence of Noah their father, and he bound them all by an oath, imprecating a curse on every one that sought to seize the portion which had not fallen (to him) by his lot. And they all said, "So be it; so be it" for themselves and their sons for ever throughout their generations till the day of judgment…" After that the land was divided by language by God. "For this reason the whole land of Shinar is called Babel, because the Lord did there confound all the language of the children of men, and from thence they were dispersed into their 26 cities, each according to his language and his nation."

I had a thought regarding languages and the nature of God. God made the themes in the kinds of animals all at once, and they diversified from what he made. From one kind of animal, we get so much variation that some people see one kind as connected with another. Languages are similar. God created, according to Jewish history, seventy languages. Thousands of dialects come from them.[97] There may even be a little breeding going on with a mixing of accents. Like a colony of ants, or a tree, God starts with the supporting structure, and it branches out from there. Alas, I'm being like Richard Lynche. Let me "return to our main intendment proceeding."

Canaan didn't go to Africa like he was supposed to. Neither did Madai go to Europe. "Madai saw the land of the sea and it did not please him, and he begged a (portion) from Ham and Asshur and Arpachshad, his wife's brother, and he dwelt in the land of Media, near to his wife's brother until this day." I'll summarize several things. Medicine has been administered since the beginning of time. "And Noah wrote down all things in a book as we instructed him concerning every kind of medicine." There was lots of violence and corruption springing up, far more detail than I need to add here. It tells of how Abram was born and about the sin of his father, Terah. Abram discerned that the idols the people worshiped were pointless. He had a revelation as he gazed into the stars. God can send rain or not, as he pleases. Abram prayed, "Deliver me from the hands of evil spirits who have dominion over the thoughts of men's hearts, and let them not lead me astray from Thee, my God. And stablish Thou me and my seed for ever that we go not astray from henceforth and for evermore." In response,

> And the Lord God said: "Open his mouth and his ears, that he may hear and speak with his mouth, with the language which has been revealed"; for it had ceased from the mouths of all the children of men from the day of the overthrow (of Babel). And I opened his mouth, and his ears and his lips, and I began to speak with him in Hebrew in the tongue of the creation. And he took the books of his fathers, and these were written in Hebrew, and he transcribed them, and he began from henceforth to study them...

I wonder if Noah had this same revelation of tongues. I wonder this in light of what Jasher says about Abram studying under Noah and Shem. It is also interesting to note that (Aram)aic is similar to the H(Eber)ew language. Aram was Eber's great uncle. Perhaps the revelation was a very broad one. Or perhaps the nation was named for the two men, and the languages were named for the nations. Perhaps only Abram had this revelation, and so he was the only one to have knowledge of the books he studied. Who knows? What I do know is that Abraham is not where we're going with this book, so we'll leave Jubilees here and move on to Jasher.

The Book of Jasher

Jasher means: The Book of the Upright. Jasher is more interesting to me than any other extra-biblical text relating to the time of Genesis. It may be completely contrived, but I would not be surprised to learn that it is a slightly corrupted form of the original text that was referred to in the Bible. Because of the corruption that seems to have happened though, I would not trust it with the same trust I give the other sixty-six widely accepted books. It is useful for history and speculation. Unlike Genesis, the text of Jasher is not easily verifiable. If you have a high standard for manuscript evidence, you really should take this book with a higher level of skepticism. Of course, with everything we're told in life, sometimes we have to be trusting. You can decide for yourself just how much trust you're willing to give. We can get clues to the trustworthiness of the message as we read it. I will summarize only the most important parts relating to the time of Noah and Shem. Let's dig in.

This is pre-flood (Chapter 2):

> And every man made his god and they bowed down to them, and the sons of men forsook the Lord all the days of Enosh and his children; and the anger of the Lord was kindled on account of their works and abominations which they did in the earth. And the Lord caused the waters of the river Gihon to overwhelm them, and he destroyed and consumed them, and he destroyed the third part of the earth, and notwithstanding this, the sons of men did not turn from their evil ways, and their hands were yet extended to do evil in the sight of the Lord.

There are several myths and legends where there was an overflowed river that wiped people out. Perhaps there was a true story associated with it. It was a flood before the Flood. Then He sent a famine "And the seed which they sowed in those days in the ground became thorns, thistles and briers; for from the days of Adam was this declaration concerning the earth, of the curse of God, which he cursed the earth, on account of the sin which Adam sinned before the Lord." This may be another example of genetic diversity at the beginning.

I feel a judgment coming. They're starting to do bad things.

> For in those days the sons of men began to trespass against God, and to transgress the commandments which he had commanded to Adam, to be fruitful and multiply in the earth. And some of the sons of men caused their wives to drink a draught that would render them barren, in order that they might retain their figures and whereby their beautiful appearance might not fade. [. . .]And the child-bearing women appeared abominable in the sight of their husbands as widows, whilst their husbands lived, for to the barren ones only they were attached.

Sometimes I wonder if the Catholic Church has the right position on contraception. Chapter 4 describes the reign of Enoch over the earth and his ascent into heaven. Corruption got worse.

> For when they sowed the ground in order that they might obtain food for their support, behold, thorns and thistles were produced which they did not sow. And their judges and rulers went to the daughters of men and took their wives by force from their husbands according to their choice, and the sons of men in those days took from the cattle of the earth, the beasts of the field and the fowls of the air, and taught the mixture of animals of one species with the other, in order therewith to provoke the Lord; and God saw the whole earth and it was corrupt, for all flesh had corrupted its ways upon earth, all men and all animals.

There's mercy in judgment, at least for those who are doing right in the sight of God (Chapter 5).

And all the sons of men who knew the Lord, died in that year before the Lord brought evil upon them; for the Lord willed them to die, so as not to behold the evil that God would bring upon their brothers and relatives, as he had so declared to do. In that time, the Lord said to Noah and Methuselah, "Stand forth and proclaim to the sons of men all the words that I spoke to you in those days, peradventure they may turn from their evil ways, and I will then repent of the evil and will not bring it." And Noah and Methuselah stood forth, and said in the ears of the sons of men, all that God had spoken concerning them. But the sons of men would not hearken, neither would they incline their ears to all their declarations.

Notice that God sent human messengers to speak this out.

Noah is going to have to take a wife if God is going to populate the world through him.

Noah went and took a wife, and he chose Naamah the daughter of Enoch, and she was five hundred and eighty years old. And Noah was four hundred and ninety-eight years old, when he took Naamah for a wife. And Naamah conceived and bare a son, and he called his name Japheth, saying, God has enlarged me in the earth; and she conceived again and bare a son, and he called his name Shem, saying, "God has made me a remnant, to raise up seed in the midst of the earth."

So we have the age of Noah's wife. This says Japheth was born first. Jubilees said Shem was.[98] Contradictions bring a little doubt on both, but I think it would be wrong to toss out everything on both sides for a few things I can't reconcile. "In his five hundred and ninety-fifth year Noah commenced to make the ark, and he made the ark in five years, as the Lord had commanded." I always thought it would take hundreds of years to build something that big. He must have had some impressive technology. Judging by the early structures on the earth, he probably did (Chapter 6).

> And thou shalt go and seat thyself by the doors of the ark, and all the beasts, the animals, and the fowls, shall assemble and place themselves before thee, and such of them as shall come and crouch before thee, shalt thou take and deliver into the hands of thy sons, who shall bring them to the ark, and all that will stand before thee thou shalt leave.

Noah didn't have to gather the animals. There was divine intervention. All he had to do was follow instructions, and God did the rest. There were many warnings of the flood.

> And on that day, the Lord caused the whole earth to shake, and the sun darkened, and the foundations of the world raged, and the whole earth was moved violently, and the lightning flashed, and the thunder roared, and all the fountains in the earth were broken up, such as was not known to the inhabitants before; and God did this mighty act, in order to terrify the sons of men, that there might be no more evil upon earth. And still the sons of men would not return from their evil ways, and they increased the anger of the Lord at that time, and did not even direct their hearts to all this. And at the end of seven days, in the six hundredth year of the life of Noah, the waters of the flood were upon the earth. And all the fountains of the deep were broken up, and the windows of heaven were opened, and the rain was upon the earth forty days and forty nights.

This is a scary prospect.

> And they called to Noah, saying, "Open for us that we may come to thee in the ark—and wherefore shall we die?" And Noah, with a loud voice, answered them from the ark, saying, "Have you not all rebelled against the Lord, and said that he does not exist? And therefore the Lord brought upon you this evil, to destroy and cut you off from the face of the earth. Is not this the thing that I spoke to you of one hundred and twenty years back, and you would not hearken to the voice of the Lord, and now do you desire to live upon earth?"

This is scarier. They were atheists. Noah wasn't very politically correct.

> And they said to Noah, "We are ready to return to the Lord; only open for us that we may live and not die." And Noah answered them, saying, "Behold now that you see the trouble of your souls, you wish to return to the Lord; why did you not return during these hundred and twenty years, which the Lord granted you as the determined period? But now you come and tell me this on account of the troubles of your souls, now also the Lord will not listen to you, neither will he give ear to you on this day, so that you will not now succeed in your wishes." And the sons of men approached in order to break into the ark, to come in on account of the rain, for they could not bear the rain upon them. And the Lord sent all the beasts and animals that stood round the ark. And the beasts overpowered them and drove them from that place, and every man went his way and they again scattered themselves upon the face of the earth.

Notice how gentle was the ebb and flow. "And the ark floated upon the face of the waters, and it was tossed upon the waters so that all the living creatures within were turned about like pottage in a cauldron." It was peaceful, like a river rapid. God kept them through the trial, but they probably noticed the destruction happening around them.

I'll skip a bit here. There's no point in copying and pasting text that you can read from the source. Much of it is similar to Genesis.

The text follows the garment given to Adam by God. It was an heirloom. Nimrod had it for a while, so Jasher spends some time on him. This is how Nimrod was born,

> And Cush the son of Ham, the son of Noah, took a wife in those days in his old age, and she bare a son, and they called his name Nimrod, saying, At that time the sons of men again began to rebel and transgress against God, and the child

> grew up, and his father loved him exceedingly, for he was the son of his old age.

Nimrod was eventually killed by Esau when he spied Nimrod hunting, and Esau sold the garment to Jacob for soup. We won't go into detail here. Nimrod lived for a long time (from Terah, Abram's father, through Esau).

Jasher continues by tracing the lineage down to Abram, who was in the house of Nimrod. There was a sign that Abram would be great, and Nimrod tried to kill him, but they switched him for another baby and hid him in a cave (Chapter 9).

> And when Abram came out from the cave, he went to Noah and his son Shem, and he remained with them to learn the instruction of the Lord and his ways, and no man knew where Abram was, and Abram served Noah and Shem his son for a long time. And Abram was in Noah's house thirty-nine years, and Abram knew the Lord from three years old, and he went in the ways of the Lord until the day of his death, as Noah and his son Shem had taught him…

Then we come to Babel. The Bible shows Babel coming shortly before Abram's story. Jasher has it the other way around. There is some weird stuff at this point in Jasher, like men turning into apes and elephants:

> And the Lord smote the three divisions that were there, and he punished them according to their works and designs; those who said, We will ascend to heaven and serve our gods, became like apes and elephants; and those who said, We will smite the heaven with arrows, the Lord killed them, one man through the hand of his neighbor; and the third division of those who said, We will ascend to heaven and fight against him, the Lord scattered them throughout the earth.

I'm not about to speculate here that apes actually came from men. Oops. I guess I just did. This is starting to sound like a Greek myth.

> And as to the tower which the sons of men built, the earth opened its mouth and swallowed up one third part thereof, and a fire also descended from heaven and burned another third, and the other third is left to this day, and it is of that part which was aloft, and its circumference is three days' walk.

There are many statements about which families moved where. Here's a sample (Franc[e]-um): "And the children of Gomer, according to their cities, were the Francum, who dwell in the land of Franza, by the river Franza, by the river Senah."

Abram gets cheeky with his father. It's pretty funny though. You will forgive the length of the quote.

> And Abram asked his father, saying, "Father, tell me where is God who created heaven and earth, and all the sons of men upon earth, and who created thee and me." And Terah answered his son Abram and said, "Behold those who created us are all with us in the house." And Abram said to his father, "My lord, shew them to me I pray thee;" and Terah brought Abram into the chamber of the inner court, and Abram saw, and behold the whole room was full of gods of wood and stone, twelve great images and others less than they without number. And Terah said to his son, "Behold these are they which made all thou seest upon earth, and which created me and thee, and all mankind." And Terah bowed down to his gods, and he then went away from them, and Abram, his son, went away with him. [. . .] And Abram saw on the day when he was sitting amongst them, that they had no voice, no hearing, no motion, and not one of them could stretch forth his hand to eat. And Abram mocked them, and said, "Surely the savory meat that I prepared has not pleased them, or perhaps it was too little for them, and for that reason they would not eat;" [. . .] and Abram sat before them all day, thinking

perhaps they might eat. […] And in the evening of that day in that house Abram was clothed with the spirit of God. And he called out and said, "Wo unto my father and this wicked generation, whose hearts are all inclined to vanity, who serve these idols of wood and stone which can neither eat, smell, hear nor speak, who have mouths without speech, eyes without sight, ears without hearing, hands without feeling, and legs which cannot move; like them are those that made them and that trust in them." And when Abram saw all these things his anger was kindled against his father, and he hastened and took a hatchet in his hand, and came unto the chamber of the gods, and he broke all his father's gods. And when he had done breaking the images, he placed the hatchet in the hand of the great god which was there before them, and he went out; […] And when Terah saw this his anger was greatly kindled, and he hastened and went from the room to Abram. And he found Abram his son still sitting in the house; and he said to him, "What is this work thou hast done to my gods?" And Abram answered Terah his father and he said, "Not so my lord, for I brought savory meat before them, and when I came nigh to them with the meat that they might eat, they all at once stretched forth their hands to eat before the great one had put forth his hand to eat. And the large one saw their works that they did before him, and his anger was violently kindled against them, and he went and took the hatchet that was in the house and came to them and broke them all, and behold the hatchet is yet in his hand as thou seest." […] and Terah said to Abram his son in his anger, "What is this tale that thou hast told? Thou speakest lies to me." […] And Abram answered his father and said to him, "And how canst thou then serve these idols in whom there is no power to do any thing? Can those idols in which thou trustest deliver thee? Can they hear thy prayers when thou callest upon them? Can they deliver thee from the hands of thy enemies, or will they fight thy battles for thee against thy enemies, that thou shouldst serve wood and stone which can neither speak nor hear? […] And forget the Lord God who made heaven and earth? […] Did

> not our fathers in days of old sin in this matter, and the Lord God of the universe brought the waters of the flood upon them and destroyed the whole earth? [...] Now therefore my father refrain from this, and bring not evil upon thy soul and the souls of thy household." And Abram hastened and sprang from before his father, and took the hatchet from his father's largest idol, with which Abram broke it and ran away.

This story is a riot! It turns out that you don't need the scientific method to figure things out. I think we can see a lot of ourselves in Terah. Of course the idols were useless for anything. You know that well, and Terah did too. Deep down, he wasn't deceived. He chose to believe the lie. Note how Terah opposed his son, even when it was clear that Abram was right. Nimrod is told, and Abram gives the same story.

Abram is in trouble. "If it pleaseth the king to do this, let him order his servants to kindle a fire both night and day in thy brick furnace, and then we will cast this man into it." Terah blamed Haran, Abram's brother. They got tossed into the fire together. Haran died, but Abram walked around in the fire.

> And Abram said to them, "Do not bow down to me, but bow down to the God of the world who made you, and serve him, and go in his ways for it is he who delivered me from out of this fire, and it is he who created the souls and spirits of all men, and formed man in his mother's womb, and brought him forth into the world, and it is he who will deliver those who trust in him from all pain." And all the kings, princes and servants gave Abram many gifts of silver and gold and pearl, and the king and his princes sent him away, and he went in peace.

Noah died during the life of Abram. "Noah died, which was the fifty-eighth year of the life of Abram" (13:9).

It then goes into a story about how the kings of Egypt began to be called *pharaoh* (Chapter 16), but I will not recount that here.

Another name is given for Shem.

> And Adonizedek king of Jerusalem, the same was Shem, went out with his men to meet Abram and his people, with bread and wine, and they remained together in the valley of Melech. And Adonizedek blessed Abram, and Abram gave him a tenth from all that he had brought from the spoil of his enemies, for Adonizedek was a priest before God.

I might be the only one to find this interesting, but it is very insightful to me. The book of Hebrews begins to make more sense as you consider that Shem was the eternal priest. I wonder if that eternal nature at all comes from the fact that he was the father of his family line. Notice that Adonai, the first part of the name given here for Shem, is also a name of God in Hebrew. The valley of Melech is the substitution for Adonai in Melchizedek, the name given for him in Hebrews. There is a lot of speculation I will not be able to get to on this, but I look forward to hearing insights from others.

I know this will be obvious to anyone who studies this time period, but I have to say it for those who do not (Chapter 17). "[T]he children of Chittim made war with the children of Tubal." All the nations of the time were named for their families. The father of the family gave them their traditions, their religion, their home, and therefore, they were also given their name based on their father. This is true in the region of Israel, and it's evident in the names given to regions across the globe. We still do it today. In the region in which I write, I can give you half a dozen names of cities that have been from their founder. Company names are for people who started them. Branches of science can be named for the founders. We leave a legacy with our children, as much as it is for our children.

You might also notice that we know a lot of the names of the nations and regions, not only in the memory of the people living there, but we also get it from the histories written about the people who had the names. You don't need to look any further than Israel (otherwise known as Jacob) to see that. Sometimes the people are remembered better than the nation that came later. Only serious historians have ever heard of the nation of Uz, and yet, he's in the table of nations in Genesis 10. You wouldn't have that if people were in the regions for hundreds of thousands of years.

The book continues on with more inbreeding: "And [Abraham] said concerning his wife, She is my sister, for such is his manner of doing when he cometh to dwell in the land in which he is a stranger" (20:20). We already knew about this one.

Abraham had the same thing happen to him as happened to the three friends of Daniel. Sodom and Gomorrah was repeated with the sons of Benjamin. Elijah was taken to heaven, just like Enoch. Abraham told two different kings that his wife was his sister. We can go two ways with this. I see two options. These stories (and many others like them) were false in their minor details and repeated so that we get them in a couple forms; thus, they are made up. The other option is that God sees fit to work in themes. You can see themes all through creation in the similarities between creatures. You can see a parallel between the coming of the flood and the Advent and future fire. When studying prophesy, we find that even when an event matched the prophesy in many details, there is still a future fulfillment in the rest of the details to come. Who knows? Maybe God, the masterful strategist, is trying to throw someone off. You can take the position you see as best in this, but let me be an advocate for repetition. How can we possibly learn if every situation is entirely different? In my opinion, the weakest position is that all the stories, being so common, are entirely fiction. There has to at least be an element of truth in all of them. They learned their lesson:

> Now, therefore, restore this woman to her husband, lest it should befall us as it did to Pharaoh king of Egypt and his subjects, and that we may not die; and Abimelech hastened and called and had Sarah called for, and she came before him, and he had Abraham called for, and he came before him.

They gave him his sister, er, wife back.

As promised, I am going to tell you what I think about the canon of scripture. You will do with it what you want, no matter what I want for you, so I give you permission to do what you want. There is only one Bible. The consistency is amazing. The power of the message is life changing. How did they come to accept which books were true and which were not? You can get a PhD in this topic, so don't think I'm exhausting it, but the short of it is that the Jews, just before Jesus' time, compiled the Old Testament. Rabbis and early church fathers, including Eusebius, made lists of books that they believed to be authoritative. The Latin Vulgate (a translation by Jerome from the Greek and Hebrew around 400 AD) pretty much solidified the accepted books of the Old and New Testaments. The last revision to that was made by the Protestant church, especially Martin Luther. The King James Version of the Bible originally had the apocrypha, which some people were starting to doubt, and when Bibles were being mass produced, many books were removed to help to offset the cost of manufacture and to satisfy the taste of the consumer.

I am certain that the books we have survived many purgings, and they are very much reliable. The books that didn't make that cut can still be reliable, but I wouldn't stake my eternal soul on them. The rest are history books, which can be dismissed at one's whim. Where do I place Jasher and Jubilees? I don't think they came through time unscathed. Jasher talks about half men, for instance. They both disagree with some aspects of the history of Diodorus and his ilk. I would let them battle the issues out one by one and see which one comes out looking stronger. I'm convinced they aren't inerrant scripture, but they're as valid as any other history of their time. The reason I even put them in the same category as Genesis is that for Jasher, if it is the same book, there are biblical references to its value and historicity. [86]

Jubilees was highly regarded throughout history and venerated by some as scripture. Both of them tell the same stories as Genesis. I'll let you use your own judgment for this. How each book was compiled, and how each author knew the intents of God, I'll let you guess at. I'll only add that every culture of that time seemed to use oracles or prophets. The people of that time were convinced that God (or the gods) was speaking through people. The Bible even talks about false prophets. I would wager that these people (both prophets and false prophets) had a lot to do with the books we have in our possession today. The short of it: trust your Bible; doubt the external sources. If you don't want to take my advice on that, get your doctorate before you doubt the Bible. Otherwise, you're just casting things out on a whim. I started and will end this chapter with this. If you cast out things of God, you are a fool.

Chapter 6

RELIGIOUS HISTORIANS

If there is one thing I want you to take away from this book, aside from the fact that the Bible is to be trusted, it is the idea that there is no such thing as prehistory. There has always been someone to tell the story of the past, both in oral and written form. We know how it started. There have always been people compiling the history for those who don't have the time to search it out. I have read what would take an average guy several years of devoted study to get through and shortened it into a couple hours of reading. I don't do it because of who I am. I do it for the sake of those who will benefit by it. I do it for you!

Now before I get too mushy, let me say that I'm not the only one who has done the grunt work. The historians of Greece and Rome from chapter three have done the same. And all of them, as I do, had worldviews. Many of them held to religions that were wrong. We can know they were wrong by the fact that they were contradicted by other historians. They can't all be right. Could some of them have been right in the way they compiled their history? Did every historian take to the idea of paganism? I think there were some that were right. They had their faults, but theirs were far fewer than their contemporaries. I will deal with two of these authors in this book. Josephus, who wrote the history of the Jews for the Romans, will come first, and Eusebius, who wrote the history of the world after Christianity became the national religion of Rome, will be last. Both of these authors wrote about times that were well beyond the scope of our study. Josephus[99] wrote about the Jews shortly after the death of Christ. You can also read Eusebius[100] if you are interested in early church history.

Josephus

Here is a summary of the *Antiquities of the Jews* by Josephus. Roman paganism was still the religion of the day.

He starts with some philosophy. If you are religious, he's about to pay you a compliment. "The reader is therefore to know, that Moses deemed it exceeding necessary, that he who would conduct his own life well, and give laws to others, in the first place should consider the divine nature ..." We who are religious have taken the first step in living life well. Once we realize there is a divine, Moses wrote to show that virtues would not automatically follow. "I mean, unless they be taught first of all, that God is the Father and Lord of all things, and sees all things, and that thence he bestows a happy life upon those that follow him; but plunges such as do not walk in the paths of virtue into inevitable miseries." Now that we know the proper place for God, we can start to live our lives in a proper way.

> Now when once he had brought them to submit to religion, he easily persuaded them to submit in all other things: for as to other legislators, they followed fables, and by their discourses transferred the most reproachful of human vices unto the gods, and afforded wicked men the most plausible excuses for their crimes; but ... that God was possessed of perfect virtue ..."

Moses used religion to make the people submit to God in all things. Others used religion for the same purpose. If you haven't reasoned your way through to these conclusions, please take a moment to see if you can find fault with his evaluation.

When starting into the origin of the world, we always start with: "Adam, which in the Hebrew tongue signifies one that is red, because he was formed out of red earth, compounded together ..." Adam has several meanings. He means dirt, red, and man.[101]

Sometimes I wonder if these people were renamed after they lived awhile. "Cain; which name, when it is interpreted, signifies a possession: the younger was Abel, which signifies sorrow..." How would you like to be named such horrible things? Perhaps they were living up to the expectations of their father. Josephus names many people from before the flood. I don't know where he gets these names, but I highly doubt he made them up. "He had indeed many other children, but Seth in particular. As for the rest, it would be tedious to name them..."

People were astrologers from the earliest times.

> They also were the inventors of that peculiar sort of wisdom which is concerned with the heavenly bodies, and their order. And that their inventions might not be lost before they were sufficiently known, upon Adam's prediction that the world was to be destroyed at one time by the force of fire, and at another time by the violence and quantity of water, they made two pillars, the one of brick, the other of stone: they inscribed their discoveries on them both, that in case the pillar of brick should be destroyed by the flood, the pillar of stone might remain, and exhibit those discoveries to mankind; and also inform them that there was another pillar of brick erected by them. Now this remains in the land of Siriad to this day.

A couple pillars that described the past flood and coming fire would be nice to have around today. It would also be nice if they were written in a tongue we could understand. If they were around during Josephus's day, they sure lasted a long time.

As you should expect by now, Noah is in this account too.

> Noah learned that the earth was become clear of the flood. So after he had staid seven more days, he sent the living creatures out of the ark; and both he and his family went out, when he also sacrificed to God, and feasted with his companions. However, the Armenians call this place, The Place of Descent; for the ark being saved in that place, its remains are shown there by the inhabitants to this day.

I'm sure lots of people are still looking for the ark. Maybe it's all around the world in the form of amulets in trash heaps.[102]

> Now all the writers of barbarian histories make mention of this flood, and of this ark; among whom is Berosus the Chaldean. [...] he goes on thus: "It is said there is still some part of this ship in Armenia, at the mountain of the Cordyaeans; and that some people carry off pieces of the bitumen, which they take away, and use chiefly as amulets for the averting of mischiefs." Hieronymus the Egyptian also, who wrote the Phoenician Antiquities, and Mnaseas, and a great many more, make mention of the same. Nay, Nicolaus of Damascus, in his ninety-sixth book, hath a particular relation about them; where he speaks thus: "There is a great mountain in Armenia, over Minyas, called Baris, upon which it is reported that many who fled at the time of the Deluge were saved; and that one who was carried in an ark came on shore upon the top of it; and that the remains of the timber were a great while preserved. This might be the man about whom Moses the legislator of the Jews wrote."

I really get excited when I see how good God is. Even when you consider the worst thing people can come up with against him, he is gracious.

> When Noah had made these supplications, God, who loved the man for his righteousness, granted entire success to his prayers, and said, that it was not he who brought the destruction on a polluted world, but that they underwent that vengeance on account of their own wickedness; and that he had not brought men into the world if he had himself determined to destroy them, it being an instance of greater wisdom not to have granted them life at all, than, after it was granted, to procure their destruction; "But the injuries," said he, "they offered to my holiness and virtue, forced me to bring this punishment upon them."

This is the debate that sci-fi authors love to write into their stories. Do our choices change the course of unfolding history? I'll let you guys try to figure that out, and what comes of it might just well be a fun movie to watch.

> Now I have for witnesses to what I have said, all those that have written Antiquities, both among the Greeks and barbarians; for even Manetho, who wrote the Egyptian History, and Berosus, who collected the Chaldean Monuments, and Mochus, and Hestieus, and, besides these, Hieronymus the Egyptian, and those who composed the Phoenician History, agree to what I here say: Hesiod also, and Hecatseus, Hellanicus, and Acusilaus; and, besides these, Ephorus and Nicolaus relate that the ancients lived a thousand years. But as to these matters, let every one look upon them as he thinks fit.

Clearly, the people of the time of Christ didn't believe it was possible to live nearly a thousand years. Lots of people insisted it was true, and there are some big names in that list.

"He [Nimrod] also said he would be revenged on God, if he should have a mind to drown the world again; for that he would build a tower too high for the waters to be able to reach!" The problem was not that man was trying to build a tower to reach where God lived. It was the arrogance of trying to say God can't get us if we take precautions. They were dumb to fight against God. Anyone who does is dumb.

Have you seen this before?

> AFTER this they were dispersed abroad, on account of their languages, and went out by colonies every where; and each colony took possession of that land which they light upon, and unto which God led them; so that the whole continent was filled with them, both the inland and the maritime countries. There were some also who passed over the sea in ships, and inhabited the islands: and some of those nations do still retain the denominations which were given them by

> their first founders; but some have lost them also, and some have only admitted certain changes in them, that they might be the more intelligible to the inhabitants. And they were the Greeks who became the authors of such mutations. For when in after-ages they grew potent, they claimed to themselves the glory of antiquity; giving names to the nations that sounded well (in Greek) that they might be better understood among themselves; and setting agreeable forms of government over them, as if they were a people derived from themselves.

I love that we don't have to theorize about this. He states it as clearly as the history that he is expounding. The nations were named for their founders; then they were renamed to make it easier for the locals to say. The Greeks embellished their histories. They did it masterfully.

I would apologize for the length of this quote, but you'll be happy to have it here. There's no reason to say I'm sorry.

> Now they were the grandchildren of Noah, in honor of whom names were imposed on the nations by those that first seized upon them. Japhet, the son of Noah, had seven sons: they inhabited so, that, beginning at the mountains Taurus and Amanus, they proceeded along Asia, as far as the river Tansis, and along Europe to Cadiz; and settling themselves on the lands which they light upon, which none had inhabited before, they called the nations by their own names. For Gomer founded those whom the Greeks now call Galatians, [Galls,] but were then called Gomerites. Magog founded those that from him were named Magogites, but who are by the Greeks called Scythians. Now as to Javan and Madai, the sons of Japhet; from Madai came the Madeans, who are called Medes, by the Greeks; but from Javan, Ionia, and all the Grecians, are derived. Thobel founded the Thobelites, who are now called Iberes; and the Mosocheni were founded by Mosoch; now they are Cappadocians. [...] Thiras also called those whom he ruled over Thirasians; but the Greeks changed the name into Thracians. [...] Now when I have

premised somewhat, which perhaps the Greeks do not know, I will return and explain what I have omitted; for such names are pronounced here after the manner of the Greeks, to please my readers; for our own country language does not so pronounce them: but the names in all cases are of one and the same ending; for the name we here pronounce Noeas, is there Noah, and in every case retains the same termination. The children of Ham possessed the land from Syria and Amanus, and the mountains of Libanus; [...] Chus; for the Ethiopians, over whom he reigned, are even at this day, both by themselves and by all men in Asia, called Chusites. The memory also of the Mesraites is preserved in their name; for all we who inhabit this country [of Judea] called Egypt Mestre, and the Egyptians Mestreans. Phut also was the founder of Libya, and called the inhabitants Phutites, from himself: [...] Canaan, the fourth son of Ham, inhabited the country now called Judea, and called it from his own name Canaan. [...] but Nimrod, the son of Chus, staid and tyrannized at Babylon, as we have already informed you. Now all the children of Mesraim, being eight in number, possessed the country from Gaza to Egypt, though it retained the name of one only, the Philistim; for the Greeks call part of that country Palestine. [...] Shem, the third son of Noah, had five sons, who inhabited the land that began at Euphrates, and reached to the Indian Ocean. For Elam left behind him the Elamites, the ancestors of the Persians. Ashur lived at the city Nineve; and named his subjects Assyrians, who became the most fortunate nation, beyond others. Arphaxad named the Arphaxadites, who are now called Chaldeans. Aram had the Aramites, which the Greeks called Syrians; as Laud founded the Laudites, which are now called Lydians. [...] Sala was the son of Arphaxad; and his son was Heber, from whom they originally called the Jews Hebrews. Heber begat Joetan and Phaleg: he was called Phaleg, because he was born at the dispersion of the nations to their several countries; for Phaleg among the Hebrews signifies division. Now Joctan, one of the sons of Heber, had these sons, Elmodad, Saleph, Asermoth, Jera, Adoram, Aizel, Decla, Ebal, Abimael,

> Sabeus, Ophir, Euilat, and Jobab. These inhabited from Cophen, an Indian river, and in part of Asia adjoining to it. And this shall suffice concerning the sons of Shem.

To summarize the quotation above, here is Genesis 10, and this is where they lived. He even mentioned what was divided during the days of Peleg. You will notice that I clipped out a lot of names from this passage. If you want to know more about this, read Josephus and the two books I have found regarding this.[103] I urge you not to pass over this section without considering what Josephus is saying. I know it can be tedious to look through the details of genealogies, but this is where the best proof is. Each nation has its own history, and each history had names similar to those given by Josephus and Genesis. This is not a coincidence.

It's really fun that Abram figured out that the stars were not gods, just by seeing their consistency. If you can use chemicals and forces to shape matter, how could you worship that same matter as a god?

> [Abram said that] if these bodies had power of their own, they would certainly take care of their own regular motions; but since they do not preserve such regularity, they make it plain, that in so far as they co-operate to our advantage, they do it not of their own abilities, but as they are subservient to Him that commands them, to whom alone we ought justly to offer our honor and thanksgiving.

I'll toss this in to help corroborate what Lynche told us earlier. "These kings had laid waste all Syria, and overthrown the offspring of the giants."

Didn't Jasher just say this?

> Now the king of Sodom met him at a certain place, which they called The King's Dale, where Melchisedec, king of the city Salem, received him. That name signifies, the righteous king: and such he was, without dispute, insomuch that, on this account, he was made the priest of God: however, they

> afterward called Salem Jerusalem. Now this Melchisedec supplied Abram's army in an hospitable manner, and gave them provisions in abundance; and as they were feasting, he began to praise him, and to bless God for subduing his enemies under him. And when Abram gave him the tenth part of his prey, he accepted of the gift: but the king of Sodom desired Abram to take the prey, but entreated that he might have those men restored to him whom Abram had saved from the Assyrians, because they belonged to him. But Abram would not do so; nor would make any other advantage of that prey than what his servants had eaten; but still insisted that he should afford a part to his friends that had assisted him in the battle.

Let's see the daddy-daughter love, or should I say selfishness. Perhaps ignorance, as this is a blatant act of ignorance.

> But his daughters, thinking that all mankind were destroyed, approached to their father, though taking care not to be perceived. This they did, that human kind might not utterly fail: and they bare sons; the son of the elder was named Moab, Which denotes one derived from his father; the younger bare Ammon, which name denotes one derived from a kinsman. The former of whom was the father of the Moabites, which is even still a great nation; the latter was the father of the Ammonites; and both of them are inhabitants of Celesyria. And such was the departure of Lot from among the Sodomites.

I probably don't need to tell you by now, but I want you to notice that the two people came before the two nations. Also, remember Adam's prophesy in light of this story. Fire destroyed their home. They were probably under the impression that Noah survived the flood, and Lot survived the fire.

To say the least, Josephus verifies the Genesis record. Let's see what Eusebius says about it. I think he has a thing or two to say about the mythical gods as well.

Eusebius

I have to say that I love Eusebius. [100] He's my favorite historian. I put his name on the bumper of my car. Now that you've heard that, you can wipe my slobber off and keep reading.

These quotes are taken from the *Cronicle* by Eusebius. Eusebius was an early church bishop, closely connected to Constantine, who both lived around 300 AD. If anyone had a reason to reject paganism, Eusebius did.

The assumption of my book is that the early history of man matters in light of the current worldview. Why did earlier church historians not look into these matters much? Maybe because one of the early experts, namely Eusebius, wrote this:

> It will help if first we remember the advice of our true master, who told his companions [Acts, 1:7]: "It is not for you to know the hours and seasons which the Father has set under his own authority." He, as our Lord and God, uttered this saying not only about the end of the world, but also, in my opinion, about all dates, to dissuade men from such pointless investigations.

He wants to argue that the point of the origin of the world is not that important. I wish I could have a debate with him on this!

Josephus wasn't the only one that didn't think highly of Greek history. Eusebius confirms:

> There is no reason to be surprised that the Greeks do not appear in the most ancient times. They have fallen into various fatal errors, and for a long time before the generation of Cadmus they were completely ignorant of writing. They say that Cadmus was the first to bring them the alphabet, from the land of the Phoenicians. And so the Egyptian in Plato's book [Timaeus, 22'B] rightly despises Solon; "O Solon," he says, "you Greeks are always children. An old Greek man is never to be found, and no-one can learn from you about ancient times."

Keep this in mind as we think about which histories to take into consideration.

He gives a bunch of king lists and dates. This is a treasure trove for people who are dedicated to detail. "That is what Berossus relates in his first book, and in the second book he lists the kings, one after another."

> Berossus, in the first book of his Babylonian History, says that he [it doesn't matter who] lived at the time of Alexander the son of Philippus, and that he transcribed the writings of many authors, which had been carefully preserved at Babylon, containing the records of over 150,000 years. These writings contain the history of heaven and the sea, of creation, and of the kings and their deeds.

Not every history points to a couple thousand years since the beginning. If you decide to believe in evolution, you can ignore all other history and use this quotation; claim that the most outrageous statements are true.

> That, according to Alexander Polyhistor, is what Berossus says in his first book. In the second book he lists the kings, one after another, and he says that the time of the ten kings, which we mentioned above, lasted for longer than 400,000 years. Anyone who believes that these writers are telling the truth about such a huge number of years should believe all the other improbable stories that they tell. Such a length of time is clearly supernatural, and is not worthy of belief, even if it is explained in a different way. And even if someone thinks that this number of years is possible, they still should not accept the statement about the dates without some further questions. If the number of rulers was sufficient to explain all these thousands of years, which are produced by their chronology, or if the writers reported the events and actions which would be expected to occur over such a length of time, then one might perhaps agree that there is some likelihood of their account being true. But as they claim that so many myriads of years were taken up by the rule of only ten men, who can doubt that these stories are merely ravings and myths?

We don't have to go too far for the answer to the riddle. "Perhaps these so-called sars were originally measured not in years, but in some very small period of time. For instance, the ancient Egyptians talked about lunar years ..." More calculations:

> So they count only ten generations from Alorus, who was the first to be called king [of the Chaldaeans], up until Xisuthrus, in whose reign the great flood occurred. In the Hebrew scriptures also, Moses declares that there were ten generations before the flood; for the Hebrews mention that number of generations, one by one, from the first man in their account up until the flood. But Hebrew history assigns about 2,000 years to these ten generations. Assyrian [history] lists the same number of generations as the book of Moses, but produces a very different total of years. It says that the ten generations lasted for 120 sars, which is the equivalent of 430,000 years. The reader who is keen to know the truth can easily understand, from what we have already said, that Xisuthrus is the same as the man who is called Noah by the Hebrews, in whose time the great flood occurred.

I'm glad he made that connection for me. It makes it more credible than if I had done it on my own.

Josephus wasn't the only one who saw people with ark amulets; Eusebius did too. "A small part of the boat, which came to rest in Armenia, can still be found in the mountains of the Cordyaei in Armenia. Some people scrape off the asphalt, which covers the boat, and use it to ward off diseases, like an amulet." Others had ark amulets too. "Abydenus, about the flood ... The inhabitants of Armenia made wooden amulets out of his ship, as a protection against poisons."

He recites details about Babel:

> The Sibyl says: "When men all spoke the same language, they built a very tall tower, so that they could climb up to heaven. However god blew a wind at them and overturned the tower. Then he gave each of them their own language,

> and so the city was called Babylon. After the flood there came Titan and Prometheus, in whose time Titan made war against Cronus."

So Titan (not the titans) made war after Babel. These mythologies do seem to mix together well.

"Abydenus … writes as follows: "Megasthenes says that Nebuchadnezzar, who was mightier than Heracles, led his armies as far as Libya and Iberia." Eusebius obviously hasn't been told that Hercules was a fable. On the other hand, he's in a better position to know. Maybe we should trust him!

> The book of Daniel tells how and in what way Nebuchadnezzar was afflicted in his mind. The Greek historians and the Chaldaeans turn his suffering to good account, by calling the madness a god who entered into him, or some demon which came to him. But this is not surprising, because it is their custom to attribute all such occurrences to a god, and to call the demons gods.

Jesus called *madness* demons too. Don't ask me, because I don't know how it all works.

First, Eusebius talks about Assyrians, who came from Asshur (a man in Genesis 10). "Castor writes about the Assyrians again in his Canons, in these words: 'First we have listed the kings of the Assyrians, starting with Belus; […] it shows that the kingdom lasted for 1,280 years.'" Then he goes into the Greek myths. "[Cephalion] adds: ' … In a later generation, when Pannyas was king of the Assyrians, the expedition of the Argonauts sailed to the river Phasis, and to Medeia of Colchis. They say that Heracles left the ship because of his love for Hylas, and wandered amongst the Cappadocians.'" He's alternating between real history and myth. By now, it goes without saying: the myth *is* history!

"The kings of the Assyrians 1. Ninus, for 52 years. They say that Ninus was the first to rule over all the inhabitants of Asia, except for the Indians. It can be shown that Abraham, the patriarch of the Hebrew nation, lived during his reign." Ninus was Nimrod.[104]

He says there were two floods. The one that happened for the Greeks was different from the one that happened for Noah.

> Therefore it is fitting, after our account of the Chaldaeans, next to relate the history of the ancient Hebrews. The description of the flood, which is recorded by the Hebrews, is very different from the stories of the Greeks, which they tell about the flood at the time of Deucalion. [The Hebrew flood] happened a long time before Ogyges and the equally large flood, which is said by the Greeks to have happened in the time of Ogyges. In all, the flood which is described by the Hebrews happened 1,200 years before the time of Ogyges, which in its turn happened 250 years before Deucalion's flood.

Some think that Ogyges was the same person as Noah, and others think their floods were different. I am not sure which is true.

Again, we're repeating ourselves. I'll just quote it and move on.

> After the flood, the human race throughout the whole world was derived from three men. Japheth was the ancestor of the inhabitants of Europe, from Mount Amanus to the western ocean. Ham was [the ancestor of the inhabitants] of Egypt, Libya and all the regions to the west in that direction. And Shem, who was the eldest brother, [was the ancestor] of the Assyrians, and all the peoples of the east.

"Nineveh is the city which is called Ninus [by the Greeks]; it was the first royal city of the Assyrians, which was founded by Asshur." And more, "Asshur was the ancestor of the Assyrians; he founded the city of Nineveh, which was later restored by Ninus the king of the Assyrians, who renamed it Ninus after his own name." Earlier, Ninus was said to be Nimrod. Maybe Nimrod stepped over into Asshur's territory. Still more repetition, "Eber, from whom the name and nation of the Hebrews was derived."

There is currently evidence that the sea was at the point of the highest mountains. They even had this evidence way back then. "We observed that, in our own times, fish had been found on top of the highest peaks of the Libanus mountains ... and the sight of them provided evidence to us that the ancient story was true."

> The first man amongst the Egyptians was Hephaestus, who discovered fire for them; he was the father of Sol [the Sun]. After him came [(?)Agathodaemon; then] Cronus; then Osiris; then Typhon the brother of Osiris; and then Horus the son of Osiris and Isis. These were the first rulers of the Egyptians.

I see little difference between the details relayed here and those given by Lynche in his book. "Ham the son of Noah became the father of Mizraim, who was also called Aegyptus ... " Ham's son was the starter of the Egyptian empire.

Eusebius has some problems with Egyptian dating.

> But if, even so, the number of years is found to be too large, then we must investigate the reason for this. Perhaps it happened that there were many kings in Egypt at the same time. They say that some of them were kings of Thinis, some of Memphis, some of Sais, and some of Ethiopia; and there were yet others in other places. And as it seems that these dynasties ruled each in its own (?) nome, it is very unlikely that they ruled in succession to each other. Rather, some of them ruled in one place, and others in another place.

I have no idea why this is in here. It's interesting though, and I'm going to let it do to you what it did to me. "In his reign the Libyans revolted from the Egyptians, but when the moon unexpectedly grew in size, they were moved by fear and surrendered again." This one too, I have no idea if it will help you. "Osorthon, whom the Egyptians called Heracles ... "

This is powerful testimony, albeit biased, that Jasher is true. It says that Egypt was being attacked from the east. Jasher says that the twelve sons of Abraham attacked Egypt. I'll let you find the Jasher text for comparison. It's too much for me to quote.

> And these six were the first rulers among them, who were all along making war with the Egyptians, and wanted gradually to eradicate them. This whole nation was styled Hyksos, that is, "shepherd-kings": for the first syllable hyk, according to the sacred dialect, denotes "a king," and sos is "a shepherd", according to the ordinary dialect; and of these is compounded Hyksos: but some say that these people were Arabians. Now in another copy it is said that this word does not denote "kings," but, on the contrary, denotes that the shepherds were "captives." For hyk, as well as hak with an aspirate, in the Egyptian language expressly denotes "captives"; and this to me seems the more probable opinion, and more in accordance with ancient history.

He found an interesting history that showed the Hebrew Exodus from Egypt. "These people, whom we have before named kings, and called shepherds also, and their descendants," as he says,

> [K]ept control of Egypt for five hundred and eleven years. "[...] A king, whose name was Misphragmuthosis, subdued the shepherds, and after driving them out of the other parts of Egypt, [...] But, despairing of taking the place by siege, he came to an agreement with them, that they should leave Egypt, and go, without suffering any harm, wherever they chose; and, after this agreement was made, they went away with all their families and possessions, not fewer in number than two hundred and forty thousand, and travelled out of Egypt, through the wilderness, toward Syria. But as they were in fear of the Assyrians, who were then the rulers of Asia, they built a city in that country which is now called Judaea; the city was large enough to contain this great number of men, and they called it Jerusalem." [...] "Ramesses [...] had an army of cavalry, and a strong navy. [...] Sethosis therefore returned back to Pelusium immediately, and recovered his kingdom again." The country was called Egypt from his name; for Manetho says, that Sethosis was himself called Aegyptus, and his brother Armais was called Danaus. [...]

> to this interval, if they are all added together, that these shepherds, as they are here called, were no other than our forefathers, who were delivered out of Egypt [...] our departure from Egypt was so ancient in time as to have preceded the siege of Troy by almost a thousand years.

If Moses predated Troy, his story really does have a bit more credibility than the histories of other nations of later times.

There's no way for me to summarize this. I'll just paste and clip so that you can see just how much circumstantial details corroborate Eusebius's source texts. Notice that there is yet another person that could have been the inspiration for the naming of Europe:

> The kings of the Sicyonians Aegialeus, for 52 years. The Peloponnese was originally called Aegialeia, after this Aegialeus. He is said to have started to rule Sicyon in the 15th year of Belus, the first king of the Assyrians. According to legend, [Belus] was the son of Poseidon and Libya.
>
> Europs, for 45 years. He reigned at the same time as Ninus, the son of Belus. "
>
> Joseph was contemporanious with Zeus, which fits -
>
> The kings of the Argives
>
> Apis, for 35 years. The country was then called Apia, after this Apis. During his reign, Joseph governed the Egyptians, as recorded by the Hebrews.
>
> Argus, the son of Zeus and Niobe, for 70 years.

If you're an athlete, this might be interesting to you. "Pelops was the first ruler of the Peloponnese, and he organised the Olympic games." Some claimed it was Hercules. "Ogygus is said to have been the first [king] of the Athenians; the Greeks relate that their great ancient flood happened in his reign." Lynche says that Ogyges is the same as Noah, but this may be a different name or simply a title. "After Ogygus, because of the great destruction caused by the flood, Attica remained without a king for 190 years, until the time of Cecrops." If Noah *was* the first king of the Athenians, this puts it all in perspective. The king list begins 190 years later (no doubt while Noah was still around):

The kings of the Athenians

Cecrops Diphyes, for 50 years. In his reign lived Prometheus, Epimetheus and Atlas. He started to rule the Athenians in the time of Triopas, the seventh king of the Argives, and Marathonius, the thirteenth king of Sicyon. At this time, Moses was prominent amongst the Hebrews, as we will show in due course. Also in his reign, the flood of Deucalion is said to have engulfed Thessaly, just as fire devastated the land of Ethiopia in the time of Phaethon.

Cranaus, an aboriginal, for 9 years.

Amphictyon, the son of Deucalion and son-in-law of Cranaus, for (?) 10 years. The deeds of the Danaidae are said to have occurred in his reign.

Erichthonius, the son of Hephaestus, who is called Erechtheus by Homerus, for 50 years. The Idaean Dactyls lived in his reign.

Pandion, the son of Erichthonius, for 40 years. The rape of Core [Persephone], and what is related about Triptolemus, occurred in his reign.

Erechtheus the son of Pandion, for 50 years. The deeds of Perseus occurred in his reign.

Cecrops, the brother of Erechtheus, for 40 years. The deeds of Dionysus occurred in his reign.

Pandion, the son of Erechtheus, for 25 years. Afterwards Pandion went into exile, and became king of Megara. The deeds of Europa, Cadmus and the Sparti occurred in his reign.

Aegeus, the son of Pandion, for 48 years. The deeds of the Argonauts and the Centaurs occurred in his reign; and Heracles held the athletic games.

[...]

Acastus, the son of Medon, for 36 years. In his reign occurred the migration of the Ionians, including Homerus, so they say. At the same time, Solomon built the temple at Jerusalem, as will be shown in due course.

[...]

Aeschylus, the son of Agamestor, for 23 years. In his twelfth year, the first Olympiad was held, in which Coroebus

> won the stadion contest. The total duration of the Athenian rulers, from Cecrops down to the first Olympiad [776 BC], was 780 years; from Ogygus to the first Olympiad, there were 970 years. From this time onwards, it is convenient to calculate dates according to the Olympiads.

Then he says, "This concludes the summary of the dates of the ancient rulers of the Athenians, as related by the older and more reliable historians." Could you imagine making up lists like this? Of course we can, but try doing it sometime. Then have someone compare your list to other sources in actual history and see if they work together. That's a science experiment!

We come to the naming of the Latins. "Romulus founded the city of the Romans ... Before this time they had been called sometimes Latins, and sometimes Aborigines, having different names at different times." Let's see what more he says about it. "At first, he was called Saturnius, and from his name the whole region was called Saturnia. Heracles had a son called Latinus, and he too ruled over the land of the Aborigines; from his name, they were called Latins." Atlas' name was attached to Italy, and Hercules' son's name was given to the Latins. Dionysius said that, "Italus came to be their king, after whom they were named Italians ... "[105] He goes on to say that the land was split in thirds.[106] With so many people taking responsibility for so many names and verification in one source and denial in others, this is enough to get mixed up in anyone's head! But take heart. If you haven't seen it already, further study will reveal that there are far more corroborating details in all the accounts of those I cite than there are contradictions. Eusebius, for one, paid close attention to the details of these records.

Thus, we end the accounts of Josephus and Eusebius. Thus, we end our reciting of history. All there is left to do is make assertions about what we have learned. That I will do in the following chapter.

Chapter 7

FINAL THOUGHTS

If you are starting on this chapter, as my wife likes to do with books, go back and read from start to finish. You will not get any evidence in this chapter.

> "He who answers a matter before he hears it is shameful and a fool."[107]

I think it is very important to take a humble posture in life. I barely even know half of what there is to know in the universe. In that half of things that I do know, I have found that others that seem to know a couple things I don't often base their knowledge on informed speculation. [108] I do too. They, like me, don't even know what is in the other half of universal knowledge. They don't have time to process the knowledge they do have, so they jump to conclusions or take claims on faith. Then something kicks on in their brain. People develop loyalty to ideas. You can work for years on someone else's preconception, and they still won't change their minds in light of solid, undisputed facts.

I used sarcasm again. Let me come clean: I don't know half of what there is to know in the universe. Judging by how many things I can count that I miss moment by moment, I probably know less than 1 percent about the world, let alone the universe and all time. We should, indeed, take a humble posture in life. On the other hand, you can learn a lot in a moment. I learned about New York City the moment I got off the plane. The people are different than they are where I live. Some of the first impressions stayed with me throughout the whole two days I was there. Other things were modified as I experienced more. Some of those perceptions are now, after two days, burned in, regardless of what the truth is. The more time passes, the less likely my perceptions of those events and the nature of New York City are going to change.

Why am I babbling about knowledge? Well, my perceptions of New York may be wrong. Because I take a humble position on the subject, all my prejudices can be changed. It could be that in the part of New York that I don't know, there is a key fact that brings me to understand that my perception, any one of them, was wrong. There are far more things I don't know about it than what I do.

That brings me to the miraculous. The thing that makes something miraculous is that we, in our experience, cannot do it, don't know how it's done, and it shouldn't be possible in light of what we think we know. Some miracles are incredible, such as a cartoon coming to life in a movie. We don't even bother to think it might be true. Other miracles are so common that we take them for granted. Wasps make nests; spiders make webs. What the heck! There are even structures made by man that we still don't know how to duplicate. Some people speculate that structures that we know to have existed would be impossible to build. They would rather believe that the structures did not exist than that we don't know how to duplicate them. It's an admission of ignorance that pride just doesn't allow for. That is why we need humility.

Is it possible that, in the half of the universe that you don't know about, miracles can happen? I agree, only some seem possible, but of the miracles to reject, why do we so readily reject that giants existed? There are midgets in the world now. It's genetic. Why deny that a man could live nearly 1,000 years? Our bodies regenerate!

I mentioned earlier that my mom had a near-death experience. There's a story behind that event. She was nearly dead, and the nurse told us to make funeral arrangements because she wouldn't be coming back. When I came back to visit her after lunch, I opted to stay in the waiting room with the kids. I had just enough faith to send my wife in to pray for her healing. She did. She asked God to heal her body. My mom told us later that, as she heard my wife praying, she was looking at her dead mother, father, brother, and sister, who were waiting for her. She knew that she was about to die. She thought that she didn't want to die, and she began to fight. They let her out of the hospital two days later. I asked her about the vision. She said that it wasn't a dream or vision. It was real. We all expected her to die, and she came back miraculously. I believe that God answered my wife's prayer, but you will believe what you want. It is an event that is shrouded in a lack of knowledge.

Whatever your position on my mom's experience, what you believe about the miraculous will determine what you accept for evidence. Can we walk on water? Can we command the wind? Can we cast out demons? You will make up your mind, and it is your prejudice that will determine what you believe about Jesus. Your decision on whether a global flood seems plausible will affect your acceptance of the mountain of historical evidence for it. Would you believe that modern computers were possible if you hadn't seen them in real life? There are too many things that you don't know to let your pride overcome you. Be humble. Be trusting! "Therefore, anyone who becomes as humble as this little child is the greatest in the Kingdom of Heaven."[109]

I want to be humble. There are too many things written in history that I have not seen for me to assume I'm absolutely right in my evaluation. Unlike some, however, I have been to New York City. My first impressions on the history I have read are powerful. It will take a lot of evidence to the contrary to convince me that what I have seen is not absolutely the way I saw it. I wager that if you look at the same evidence as I have, with the same attitude, you might just see it the same way I did. We may not know everything there is to know, but we have, at least, started reading history. We know enough to see that modern authors have been spinning the data. They're not telling the story correctly. We know enough to see that the modernist story was tainted or is blatantly false. Whether we accept this history is not a stance made by evidence but by choice. For some, it won't matter how much evidence I show that Noah was a real man and that Hercules can prove it. They hate God, and any evidence that takes that hate down a notch will not be permitted. Others are so convinced that God and Noah are real that they think this kind of a book is worthless to them. I'm not like either of these people, and I hope that those who are like me can use this book to make an informed decision about what to think about the nature of the universe.

If you have a high standard for truth, good! I think that's wonderful. Keep an equally high standard for measuring something false. Otherwise, you'll be staring the truth in the face and not be able to see it. You may not be able to accept the testimony of Annio or Lynche, but what reason is there to toss out the testimony of Diodorus or Strabo? There is a helpful story given by Bill Cooper in his book, *After the Flood.* For years, many thought that a document was made up because they didn't have the source document that it was translated from. I'll let him finish the story.

> On Wednesday 7th November 1917, Flinders Petrie, a renowned archaeologist of the day, addressed the assembled members of the British Academy. [...] The ancient book to which he drew attention was known to him as the Tysilio Chronicle [...] It is written in medieval Welsh, and is, as its colophon reveals, a translation that was commissioned by the same Walter of Oxford who commissioned Geoffrey of Monmouth to translate a certain very ancient British book into Latin. It is, in fact, a translation from early British into medieval Welsh of the same source-material used by Geoffrey, and is an answer to all those learned critics who have stated with such emphasis over the years that Geoffrey of Monmouth was lying when he claimed to have translated such a book.[110]

Notice that the historians before 1917 claimed that Geoffrey was lying. The only reason they had to reject the text is that they didn't like what it contained. They decided against him without proof and were wrong.

Let's Tie Up Some Loose Ends

There is a lot of incest in this book. Hercules fornicated everywhere he went. "From this campaign Heracles returned into Arcadia, and as he stopped at the home of Aleos the king he lay secretly with his daughter Augê, brought her with child, and went back to Stymphalus." [43] I want to mention that I do not think fornication is okay. I think that with a pure genetic line, incest can be fine, and that is the way things were, but that is not the way things are; we can't be doing that anymore. Also, the heroes of history didn't always have the greatest morals. Don't look to historical figures to figure out what to do in life. Look toward the Bible for that! Still, as with all my advice, you can take it or leave it.

You may ask, "Why have I never heard this before?" I would answer, "Why haven't you told anyone any of this before?" With history, we can only know what we are told. We even take our birthday on faith. Until we're told some things, either by forensics or word of mouth, we don't even know where to start.

Let's do a thought experiment. I have tried this on dozens of people. How many times have you heard the Christmas song, "Deck the Halls?" You probably have the lyrics memorized. Have you ever actually taken the time to understand the lyrics? "Deck the halls with boughs of holly. 'Tis the season to be jolly. Don we now our gay apparel. Troll the ancient yuletide carol." Now, unless you're like me, an utter nerd, you've have no idea what this means. Look it up! I'll wait… Did you start into the second verse? Why didn't you know this before now? You have always known the lyrics. You have always had a dictionary. Well, it turns out that most people don't bother to look. It is the same for history. Fifty years ago, we could go to a library and read Strabo and Eusebius. We could search out all the information we could find regarding early man and connect the dots. Most people didn't even try. Only one person in a dozen is curious. Only one person in a hundred is motivated enough for a cursory glance. One in ten thousand spends time on it. There just aren't enough interested parties to keep the stories alive.

Why haven't you heard about this before? It's because you haven't looked. That's not to say that you're not living your life the right way. You may well be. There are a lot of things to look for answers to. Only you can decide if you have been squandering your time. Likewise, only you can decide if this information is worth looking into further. You are the one that has to advance this message. Otherwise, half a dozen people may run across my book (or more likely, Lynche's book) in the next hundred or so years, and they'll be the only ones with this information. Their neighbors will be asking why they hadn't heard it before now. As with genetics, we can't have grandchildren without first having children. Don't let this information stop with you.

I told you that I would tell you why I thought people moved from the true history of Noah to this tripe we call *paganism.* Let me admit that I don't have a definitive answer. I am speculating. I blame three things. The first and most likely culprit is the rebellion of Ham. Not only did he and his sons break treaties in settling in land that wasn't theirs, but they made conquests early. Osiris ruled in Italy (Japheth's territory), and Nimrod ruled in Asia Minor (Shem's territory). The second is that the languages were divided at Babel. Nothing serves better in creating confusion than a lack of communication. The third is time. When you take the language in isolation, it probably couldn't have wiped out the knowledge that Noah likely dispensed to his children. With time, the notions that were given by Noah, mixed with those false notions given through Ham, resulted in corruption. In the end, we are left to decide which account to trust.

So why should we trust the Hebrews? Another question that is very similar would be: why shouldn't we believe all the other crazy things that the gods of Greece did if we're going to believe Genesis? Well, this isn't a simple answer. I've been looking into this my whole life. I'm still looking into it. I will give you a few ideas though. The first reason is that, of all the ancient history that I have ever encountered, Israel's account seems the most plausible and least embellished. If you know of another that is of equal or greater worth, I encourage you to send it to me. I would be happy to read it and hopefully discuss why you would say it is better than what I have accepted. Another reason is that Jasher says that Abram studied under Noah and Shem. There is tremendous authority in being one of the few to have the wisest people in the world to train you in what they know. They also have the miracles of Moses on their side and archaeological evidence supporting their every claim, even when the claim was doubted twenty years earlier.

The converse is evidence too. With all the histories from that age supporting each other, it seems prudent to pick one or more to accept. Would you rather decide for the Egyptian version of events? And my last support, which is the strongest one, Jesus claimed the Jewish history as his own. If you haven't looked into Jesus, then do it! Start with the book of Matthew, in the Bible. The Bible is free all over the Internet. His arrival was foretold. He worked miracles. Jesus was more than a man. He claimed to be God in a body. He spoke of the events of Genesis as though they were true. With the eternal God on this side of history, there's no point in arguing against it.

I also want to make it clear that, aside from Christianity, the only perspective that almost claimed my soul was the theory of evolution. I didn't think it was true because it sounded plausible; I thought it might be true because so many smart people bought into it. I spent a long time looking at this idea. The more I see, the more I'm convinced that it is impossible. It could never happen. Even if Christianity is not true, evolution is impossible. It sounds good on the surface, but once you start looking into the details of what has to change and how likely that is to happen, you come to realize that it is not a rational belief. At the end of the book, I'll give you a slew of resources that will help you to agree with me.

I have one final instruction for you. There is a difference between a denial and a refutation. With a denial, you might have evidence to counter or even to remove some of the certainty that once existed with an argument, but it is not conclusive. With a refutation, all doubt is removed. I freely admit that I have not given evidence that cannot be doubted. I did not refute the opposition. The reverse is true as well. I have never seen a refutation of any of this evidence. Everything from chapter two has been denied by highly educated people. Both sides have been debating the issues for thousands of years. Historians have been denying the data presented in chapters three through six for as long as there has been data to deny.

My instruction is this. You need to be careful that you are not accepting a piece of evidence as a refutation because someone you admire is convinced of it. Don't believe a smarter friend simply because they're smart. Ask yourself if the evidence really proves the case. I have found that when someone tells me that something is not true, even when I know it to be, it does one of two things. I'm either humble or proud. It will cause me to doubt my resolve, or it will harden it. In the past, I have given evidence and gotten this response, "Well, that's not very convincing." The evidence doesn't change, and yet, my confidence in it is lessened. Conversely, when someone tells me that something is true, my confidence in it increases. Know this about the human mind. If you are aware of it, it will be far less likely to make you its victim.

It would be wonderful to have someone to help me correct my mistakes. I'm sure there are many. I enjoy learning, so if I am ignorant at points, I would love to learn more. That said, I have read Greek, Roman, Jewish, Chinese, and many other histories throughout the world, and I have not found anything in any of them that is irreconcilable with my worldview. In fact, I find that almost all of it contributes to my confidence in it. I'm not sure any other worldview can make such a claim. Before you let any one bit of evidence convince you, I urge you to think it through. Do research before you make your choice. Peer pressure or brain chemistry might just make it impossible to change your mind later.

In Summary

Evolution is impossible. History is indifferent to the age of the universe, and an old earth has too many problems to be likely. Man came into history too quickly to have been around for two hundred thousand years. The historians of Greece and Rome thought that the myths of Homer and other poets were true history. Even the Jewish and Christian historians thought the same. There were genealogies (and still are today) that link all men back to Noah. The gods of the ancients were deified men. The way of the polytheists is this. The gods had particular attributes, such as Mars being the god of war. They had corresponding celestial bodies and sometimes constellations. They always have a birth story, often stemming from life among men. Thus, they often had corresponding lands, nations, rivers, and skills that were given their name. People would pray to the god that would give them the most sympathy, based on their interests. They used oracles and prophets to discern the will of the gods. The gods were given attributes, both with the stars and with the properties of our physical surroundings.

Egyptians, Libyans, Ethiopians, Indians, Persians, Greeks, Romans, and Barbarians of many other origins (even to Japan) all attested to the gods of Rome or similar. Paganism is found throughout the world. There are many other similarities between nations around the world, such as their desire to divine the stars. From those stars, they get a year (solar revolution), a month (lunar revolution), and from their common heritage, they get a seven-day week. Most have flood stories and men being formed from dirt. There is a common agreement that the world is divided into three continents, when it makes little sense to separate Europe from Asia. Every article of evidence points to a population of the earth in little spots, not in waves from one spot. We even have the names of the people that founded the nations that exist today. We know where the names of many of the rivers, seas, and nations, and even continents, come from, having had them written down in the ancient histories. Each nation, being separated, was subject to inbreeding and, thereby, a decrease in genetic diversity. Every generation since the beginning has degenerated a little more than the one that came before it. A little more information is lost with every child that is born.[111] We know that Noah was historically real and, therefore, that the judgment on the people of his age was real. It was said that Adam and many others prophesied that there will be a burning of the earth because of its iniquity. History will repeat itself. Maybe you've heard that a day is as a thousand years to the Lord. Maybe you haven't read the context of that passage.

> First of all, you must understand that in the last days scoffers will come, scoffing and following their own evil desires. They will say, "Where is this 'coming' he promised? Ever since our fathers died, everything goes on as it has since the beginning of creation." But they deliberately forget that long ago by God's word the heavens existed and the earth was formed out of water and by water. By these waters also the world of that time was deluged and destroyed. By the same word the present heavens and earth are reserved for fire, being kept for the day of judgment and destruction of ungodly men. But do not forget this one thing, dear friends: With the Lord a day is like a thousand years, and a thousand years are like a day. The Lord is not slow in keeping his promise, as some understand slowness. He is patient with you, not wanting anyone to perish, but everyone to come to repentance.[112]

Have you ever met someone who laughs at those who believe in Noah? They say that they're not convinced that Jesus, if he even existed, is ever going to come back. They say that every generation thought that Jesus was coming back, and he hasn't. They say that the present is the key to the past. Well, we have a clue. Jesus might just be waiting for you to repent! Peter thought it was important to point out that a day is like a thousand years to God. Why do we have a seven-day week? God works in themes, doesn't he? If James Ussher is to be trusted, the earth is about six thousand years old. For the Hebrews, a day begins with evening. Revelation tells us that there is going to be a thousand year peace, or rest. It is speculation, but could it be that we're just about to see the sunset, ushering in the seventh "day"? There is one more clue I have for you. This one is from the prophet Paul.

> But mark this: There will be terrible times in the last days. People will be lovers of themselves, lovers of money, boastful, proud, abusive, disobedient to their parents, ungrateful, unholy, without love, unforgiving, slanderous, without self-control, brutal, not lovers of the good, treacherous, rash, conceited, lovers of pleasure rather than lovers of God—having a form of godliness but denying its power. Have nothing to do with them. They are the kind who worm their way into homes and gain control over weak-willed women, who are loaded down with sins and are swayed by all kinds of evil desires, always learning but never able to acknowledge the truth. Just as Jannes and Jambres opposed Moses, so also these men oppose the truth—men of depraved minds, who, as far as the faith is concerned, are rejected. But they will not get very far because, as in the case of those men, their folly will be clear to everyone.[113]

That is an uncanny description of our day.

You may ask, "What do I do with all this?" This question is very similar to the question everyone should ask, "Why are we here?" It is clear to me that God is a relational being. He made us to be relational creatures. He wasn't content to let us be fully dependent on him, making each of us from dirt and breathing into us all the breath of life. We were conceived by parents. We were raised and nurtured by them. We need them, and they need us. It is the divine design, and it really is divine. God didn't speak to us all individually, nor did he give us all the same endowments and skills. He made us dependant on each other. He gave prophets. He created builders and artists. He created teachers and skeptics. God could have built it all for us and plugged us into a bliss maker. That was not his design. He would much rather have us working for each other and him, and that is what we should aim to do. There's more.

We don't do what we are supposed to do. Adam didn't trust God. We're no better. We killed prophets and ignored truth. We hurt, lie, and steal. We are not quick to forgive. We go our own way and do not become any kinder as the years pass. We need him to teach us. We need him to forgive us. We need him to mend what we have broken and give back what we have stolen. Some of us do, and he is very quick to forgive. He teaches us how he designed us to live. Others make themselves blind. They become willingly ignorant. We have no excuses. Knowledge of Noah's historicity, or even of God's righteousness, does not produce goodness in people. Adam sinned. Ham went his own way. God, in his infinite wisdom, found it necessary to destroy those who did not adopt his ways, meaning the ways of righteousness. He drowned them all! And he has promised to do it again, with fire next time, when we do not take heed. I don't want this to happen to you.[114]

Open your eyes. Stop making excuses. Live the life you were designed for. Most of all, accept the plan he set up in order to bring the mending. Since the beginning of history, people have been sacrificing animals on altars to please their gods. That institution was set up by God with Adam. It was a pointer to the ultimate sacrifice of his Son. All the attempts by man to appease God didn't remove sin. It was only the sacrifice that God provided for us that changed us in our hearts. God can decide not to accept our offerings, and likewise, we can decide not to accept his. It is our own choice, but I hope you can see the value in the invaluable.

APPENDIX: A LOT OF EXTRA MATERIAL

I read a lot when preparing for this book. I wrote a bunch of notes, and when the book was compiled, I was left with interesting things that have little to do with the purpose of the book. Often, when I only needed one reference, I found several. I'm just dumping all that information here. Hopefully, you will find it useful.

Gods and Genealogies

I will lay out in text what would probably be more helpful in a chart. I will pass on that joyous task to you instead.

Virgil wrote of the first gods:

> Our founder Dardanus, as fame has sung,
> And Greeks acknowledge, from Electra sprung:
> Electra from the loins of Atlas came;
> Atlas, whose head sustains the starry frame.
> Your sire is Mercury, whom long before
> On cold Cyllene's top fair Maia bore.
> Maia the fair, on fame if we rely,
> Was Atlas' daughter, who sustains the sky.
> Thus from one common source our streams divide;
> Ours is the Trojan, yours th' Areadian side.
> [...]
> Then Saturn came, who fled the pow'r of Jove,
> Robb'd of his realms, and banish'd from above.
> The men, dispers'd on hills, to towns he brought,
> And laws ordain'd, and civil customs taught,[115]

The start of the gods was, according to Diodorus, with the Egyptians.

> And since Egypt is the country where mythology places the origin of the gods, where the earliest observations of the stars are said to have been made, and where, furthermore, many noteworthy deeds of great men are recorded, we shall begin our history with the events connected with Egypt.[116]

I tend to think that all these myths were history and that there was no originator. Saying that one group had the story first is as good as saying that it happened there. I don't think it's possible to attribute the start of all the gods to one region. He continues with the earliest of gods. Osiris (sun, also called Dionysus and Sirius) and Isis (moon) were first and eternal gods, then Zeus (gave us spirit), then Athena (gave us air, daughter of Zeus). He then gives a slew of clues.

> And besides these there are other gods, they say, who were terrestrial, having once been mortals, but who, by reason of their sagacity and the good services which they rendered to all men, attained immortality, some of them having even been kings in Egypt. Their names, when translated, are in some cases the same as those of the celestial gods, while others have a distinct appellation, such as Helius, Cronus, and Rhea, and also the Zeus who is called Ammon by some, and besides these Hera and Hephaestus, also Hestia, and, finally, Hermes. Helius was the first king of the Egyptians, his name being the same as that of the heavenly star. Some of the priests, however, say that Hephaestus was their first king, since he was the discoverer of fire and received the rule because of this service to mankind; [. . .]Then Cronus became the ruler, and upon marrying his sister Rhea he begat Osiris and Isis, according to some writers of mythology, but, according to the majority, Zeus and Hera, whose high achievements gave them dominion over the entire universe. From these last were sprung five gods, one born on each of the five days which the Egyptians intercalate; the names of these children were Osiris and Isis, and also

> Typhon, Apollo, and Aphroditê; and Osiris when translated is Dionysus, and Isis is more similar to Demeter than to any other goddess; and after Osiris married Isis and succeeded to the kingship he did many things of service to the social life of man. […] Osiris, they say, founded in the Egyptian Thebaid […] some named it Thebes. […] Osiris, they add, also built a temple to his parents, Zeus and Hera …

It is interesting that there was a nation named after Ammon, son of Lot. Maybe they mixed his line up with Zeus. Also, Osiris was the son of Zeus in this list.

> For Osiris was laughter-loving and fond of music and the dance; consequently he took with him a multitude of musicians, among whom were nine maidens who could sing and were trained in the other arts, these maidens being those who among the Greeks are called the Muses; and their leader (hegetes), as the account goes, was Apollo, who was for that reason also given the name Musegetes. As for the Satyrs, they were taken along in the campaign because they were proficient in dancing and singing and every kind of relaxation and pastime; for Osiris was not warlike, nor did he have to organize pitched battles or engagements, since every people received him as a god because of his benefactions. In Ethiopia he instructed the inhabitants in agriculture and founded some notable cities, and then left behind him men to govern the country and collect the tribute.

So we have the muses, and Osiris wasn't warlike.

> Now when Osiris arrived at the borders of Ethiopia, he curbed the river by dykes on both banks, so that at flood-time it might not form stagnant pools over the land to its detriment, but that the flood-water might be let upon the countryside, in a gentle flow as it might be needed, through gates which he had built. After this he continued his march through Arabia along the shore of the Red Sea as far as India and the limits of the inhabited world. He also founded not a few cities in India …

They were travelers, especially Osiris. They were engineers. Osiris was the result of fornication. "The fatherhood of the child he attributed to Zeus, in this way magnifying Osiris and averting slander from his violated daughter. The tale was given out among the Greeks to the effect that Semelê, the daughter of Cadmus, was the mother of Osiris by Zeus." This guy was his own father! We saw this earlier in this paragraph. Either we're wrong to say that Osiris was Zeus or the mix up was deeply entrenched. Judging by how many other conflicts there are in these stories, I lean toward them being confused in this account. Dionysus was a Greek. "[T]hat Dionysus had been born of Semelê and Zeus. […] They were glad to receive the god as a Greek, which, as has been said, is what he was considered to be." The people of that age got all the gods mixed up.

> For the same goddess is called by some Isis, by others Demeter, by others Thesmophorus, by others Selenê, by others Hera, while still others apply to her all these names. Osiris has been given the name Sarapis by some, Dionysus by others, Pluto by others, Ammon by others, Zeus by some, and many have considered Pan to be the same god; and some say that Sarapis is the god whom the Greeks call Pluto."

Look at this one. "And on the stele of Osiris the inscription is said to run: 'My father is Cronus, the youngest of all the gods, and I am Osiris the king.'" If the "I" in there is actually Osiris, meaning he made his own monument, deification of the gods began very early indeed. Cronus (Ham) married his sister Rhea, and both were children of Noah. That means that Ham was the youngest, if any of this is to be believed. Ham was the bad son that created bad religion, took over all of Europe, and spread it everywhere. If you're interested in the relationships of the gods, look at Hyginus, especially the beginning.[117]

Diodorus, in his third book, recounts what the Atlantians thought about the early gods. He speaks of them in the present tense.

> [I]t does not differ greatly from the myths of the Greeks. Now the Atlantians, dwelling as they do in the regions on the edge of the ocean [...] This is the account given in their myth: Their first king was Uranus, and he gathered the human beings, who dwelt in scattered habitations, within the shelter of a walled city and caused his subjects to cease from their lawless ways and their bestial manner of living [...] because they thought that he had been so intimately acquainted with the risings and the settings of the stars [...] they proclaimed him to be the king of the universe. To Uranus, the myth continues, were born forty-five sons from a number of wives, and, of these, eighteen, it is said, were by Titaea, each of them bearing a distinct name, but all of them as a group were called, after their mother, Titans. Titaea [...] was changed to Gê. [...] Rhea, whom some also named Pandora. [... Rhea's husband killed Helius, her son, and Selenê killed herself, and they are the sun and the moon ...] and as for their mother, they considered her to be a goddess and erected altars to her ...

Later, he says more in the same book.

> [T]he kingdom was divided among the sons of Uranus, the most renowned of whom were Atlas and Cronus. Of these sons Atlas received as his part the regions on the coast of the ocean, and he not only gave the name of Atlantians to his peoples but likewise called the greatest mountain in the land Atlas. They also say that he perfected the science of astrology and was the first to publish to mankind the doctrine of the sphere; and it was for this reason that the idea was held that the entire heavens were supported upon the shoulders of Atlas [...] Atlas, the myth goes on to relate, also had seven daughters [...] Maea, Electra, Taÿgetê, Steropê, Meropê, Halcyonê, and the last Celaeno. These daughters lay with the most renowned heroes and gods and thus became the first ancestors of the larger part of the race of human beings, giving birth to those who, because of their high achievements, came to be called gods and heroes; Maea the eldest, for instance,

> lay with Zeus and bore Hermes […] The Atlantides were also called "nymphs" […] Cronus, the brother of Atlas, the myth continues, who was a man notorious for his impiety and greed, married his sister Rhea, by whom he begat that Zeus who was later called "the Olympian." But there had been also another Zeus, the brother of Uranus and a king of Crete, who, however, was far less famous than the Zeus who was born at a later time. Now the latter was king over the entire world, whereas the earlier Zeus, who was lord of the above-mentioned island, begat ten sons who were given the name of Curetes; and the island he named after his wife Idaea, and on it he died and was buried, and the place which received his grave is pointed out to our day. […] Cronus, they say, was lord of Sicily and Libya, and Italy as well, and, in a word, established his kingdom over the regions to the west […] Zeus, however, the son of Cronus, emulated a manner of life the opposite of that led by his father, and since he showed himself honourable and friendly to all, the masses addressed him as "father." As for his succession to the kingly power, some say that his father yielded it to him of his own accord, but others state that he was chosen as king by the masses because of the hatred they bore toward his father, and that when Cronus made war against him with the aid of the Titans, Zeus overcame him in battle, and on gaining supreme power visited all the inhabited world, conferring benefactions upon the race of men. He was pre-eminent also in bodily strength and in all the other qualities of virtue and for this reason quickly became master of the entire world. And in general he showed all zeal to punish impious and wicked men and to show kindness to the masses. In return for all this, after he had passed from among men he was given the name of Zên …

The account given here and the one given by Lynche seem to be compatible, for the most part. Maybe the critics of Annio hadn't read Diodorus. If I had to guess what happened, Ham (Cronus) was tyrannical, tromped around Europe when he should have been in Africa, and wasn't well liked by the people.

When his son, Osiris (Zeus), who didn't like his father at all, came into the region to bestow his wisdom and benefactions, he was elected as their leader. Lynche says that Ham was killed by Nimrod. I think a case can be made that Zeus was Nimrod. The problem with that is that Nimrod never had a son named Hercules. Mizraim had Lud (or Libya), where Hercules was originally a prince. This leads me to think that they joined forces to overthrow Cronus, which is in numerous accounts.

When did all these people live?

> Orpheus was contemporary with Heracles, both of them living one hundred years before the period of the Trojan War; and as I read in the work of Orpheus On Stones, where he speaks about himself, he says that he lived just a little after Helenus, and that Homer was one generation after Helenus. And Homer, according to Dionysius the writer of cycles, is said to have lived at the time of two expeditions, that against Thebes and the one which the Greeks undertook on behalf of Helen. And Diodorus agrees with Dionysius, as do countless others.[118]

A keen eye will notice that Diodorus is referencing his own material. Well, that's because it's not actually Diodorus, but the compiled fragments of his work. It seems like Homer goes back to the time of Helen (or Troy), and Hercules was around a hundred years before that. I wouldn't take this one quote too far. Compare lots of dates to get a better chronology.

He lists some children of Zeus.

> To Zeus also were born, they say, the goddesses Aphroditê and the Graces, Eileithyia and her helper Artemis, the Hours, as they are called, Eunomia and Dikê and Eirenê, and Athena and the Muses, and the gods Hephaestus and Ares and Apollo, and Hermes and Dionysus and Heracles.[57]

Apparently, Zeus was married to Europe. "Minos, the son of Zeus and Europê"[57]

There are lots of names in Diodorus's third book. [45] If you are researching the gods, you should get the information directly from there.

The Titans were of Cronus.

> The Titans numbered six men and five women, being born, as certain writers of myths relate, of Uranus and Gê, but according to others, of one of the Curetes and Titaea, from whom as their mother they derive the name they have. The males were Cronus, Hyperion, Coeus, Iapetus, Crius, and Oceanus, and their sisters were Rhea, Themis, Mnemosynê, Phoebê, and Tethys. [57]

Many of the gods were called by several names. I'll list a few. "The Egyptians, for example, say that Demeter and Isis are the same…" [57] "Venus is called Mylitta by the Assyrians." [63] The Greeks and Egyptians had sets that were comparable to each other.

> The Greeks regard Hercules, Bacchus, and Pan as the youngest of the gods. With the Egyptians, contrariwise, Pan is exceedingly ancient, and belongs to those whom they call "the eight gods," who existed before the rest. Hercules is one of the gods of the second order, who are known as "the twelve"; and Bacchus belongs to the gods of the third order, whom the twelve produced. [49]
> They call Apollo, in their language, Horus; Ceres they call Isis; Diana, Bubastis. [49]

Let's talk about Hercules.

> In the case of Heracles, for instance, it is generally agreed that during the whole time which he spent among men he submitted to great and continuous labours and perils willingly, in order that he might confer benefits upon the race of men and thereby gain immortality… [53]

If he sought to gain his life, he will have lost it, according to Jesus (Luke 17:33). But I digress. There were three Herculeses.

Every time I see this distinction, the descriptions are different. This one seems like it might be true, however. It's a bit different from the history Lynche tells.

> "For there had been two persons of an earlier period who had borne the same name [Heracles], the most ancient Heracles who, according to the myths, had been born in Egypt, had subdued with arms a large part of the inhabited world, and had set up the pillar which is in Libya, and the second, who was one of the Idaean Dactyls of Crete and a wizard with some knowledge of generalship, was the founder of the Olympic Games; but third and last, who was born of Alcmenê and Zeus a short time before the Trojan War, visited a large part of the inhabited world while he was serving Eurystheus and carrying out his commands. And after he had successfully completed all the Labours he also set up the pillar which is in Europe, but because he bore the same name as the other two and pursued the same plan of life as did they, in the course of time and upon his death he inherited the exploits of the more ancient persons of the name, as if there had been in all the previous ages but one Heracles.

You know, he may not have been eternal, but if some of the stories about him are to be believed, he hung out with a very ancient crowd. "Hercules was sent to kill the eagle which was eating out Prometheus' heart. When it was killed, Prometheus after thirty thousand years was freed from Mount Caucasus."[119] I'm just kidding; I don't believe this story. Hey, look, the merciless grandson of Hercules: "There was a certain king of Sardis, Candaules by name, whom the Greeks called Myrsilus. He was a descendant of Alcaeus, son of Hercules." [63] He's a merciless candle. He wasn't the only one descended from Hercules. "The Heraclides, descended from Hercules..." [63] The way that guy reproduced, I'm surprised we're not all descended from him.

For even more information about Hercules, try Diodorus, book four. [43]

Dionysus was the son of Zeus. "Now when Dionysus was on the point of setting out against Cronus and his force was already passing out of Nysa, his guardian Aristaeus, the myth relates, offered a sacrifice and so was the first man to sacrifice to him as to a god." [45] Why was the son of Zeus warring with Cronus? The circular nature of these relationships leads me to conclude that Zeus was his own father, being that he was both Zeus and Dionysus. Dionysus was the son of Zeus, who killed his mother with a show of thunder. Lynche says that Zeus and Dionysus were brothers, but Dionysus adopted Zeus. They were confused. Dionysus invented beer and wine. "Some writers of myths, however, relate that there was a second Dionysus who was much earlier in time than the one we have just mentioned. For according to them there was born of Zeus and Persephonê a Dionysus who is called by some Sabazius ... " [43] Maybe he named his son after himself, creating confusion. Zeus had enough sons that it could have happened.

We haven't talked much about Poseidon, but he had kids who had islands named after them.

> Poseidon, the myth continues, when he had grown to manhood, became enamoured of Halia, the sister of the Telchines, and lying with her he begat six male children and one daughter, called Rhodos, after whom the island was named. And at this period in the eastern parts of the island there sprung up the Giants, as they were called; and at the time when Zeus is said to have subdued the Titans, he became enamoured of one of the nymphs, Himalia by name, and begat by her three sons, Spartaeus, Cronius, and Cytus. [57]

That does lend to the fact that all of the gods were once mortal. It is interesting how involved they get when talking about these gods.

> But as regards the ancestry of Triopas there is disagreement among many of the historians and poets; for some have recorded that he was the son of Canachê, the daugh-

ter of Aeolus and Poseidon, but others that he was born of Lapithes, the son of Apollo, and Stilbê, the daughter of Peneius. [57]

This makes me think that there may actually be evidence they can give to support their assertions. Otherwise, why disagree with each other? I have seen people get excited over fiction before, so maybe this isn't good evidence.

The devil had a son: "When Ceyx, son of Hesper (also called Lucifer) and Philonis, had perished in a shipwreck"[120] Was that pronounced "sex"? Who had Ceyx? Lucifer wasn't the only one that became a star.[121] "Perseus, son of Jove and Danae, put among the stars; Arcas, son of Jove and Callisto, placed among the stars"[122] Look, it's a bird! "Phoenix set out for Africa, and there remained. From this the Africans are called Phoenicians."[123]

All this is just because I thought it was interesting as I read it, and I wrote it down. There were whole chapters and sections that I didn't sift through. I tossed out a whole bunch of stuff I did write down. There were books I heard the name of that weren't translated to English. A scholar could easily study this for a very long time, and the thought that it might have been our own history might provide the motivation for someone to live theirs toward that end. Likewise, someone could easily use this information to understand the relationships between the heroes of that age.

A Catastrophic World

There are lots of little bits of information that you can pick up while reading these historians about the catastrophic state of the world. When you put the clues together, you can sometimes speculate in an educated fashion about what might happen to the earth in the future. This is just for fun, and I don't expect anyone to use this stuff to support their science.

Atlantiens were still around during the time of Diodorus or so he makes us believe. "Such, then, are the myths which are told about Mother of the God both among the Phrygians and by the Atlantians who dwell on the coast of the ocean." [45] One could speculate that the sea level rose early on. It would explain what he says about this: "The ancient mythographers, that is, say that Sicily was originally a peninsula, and that afterward it became an island..." This one sounds a lot closer to myth than to reality, but you can probably get a few gems out of it.

> At a later time, the myth continues, the Telchines, perceiving in advance the flood that was going to come, forsook the island and were scattered. Of their number Lycus went to Lycia and dedicated there beside the Xanthus river a temple of Apollo Lycius. And when the flood came the rest of the inhabitants perished,—and since the waters, because of the abundant rains, overflowed the island, its level parts were turned into stagnant pools—but a few fled for refuge to the upper regions of the island and were saved, the sons of Zeus being among their number. Helius, the myth tells us, becoming enamoured of Rhodos, named the island Rhodes after her and caused the water which had overflowed it to disappear. But the true explanation is that, while in the first forming of the world the island was still like mud and soft, the sun dried up the larger part of its wetness and filled the land with living creatures, and there came into being the Heliadae, who were named after him, seven in number, and other peoples who were, like them, sprung from the land itself. [57]

Of course, Philo thinks the opposite is true, because he sees historical evidence that land came out of water in places.[124] He also sees that this perspective may be true. He speaks about it in depth.

> "Do not look only at the islands which have risen up out of the sea [...] but look rather at the contrary effects: consider how many districts on the main-land, not only such as were near the coast, but even such as were completely inland, have been swallowed up by the waters; and consider how great

a portion of land has become sea and is now sailed over by innumerable ships." Are you ignorant of the celebrated account which is given of that most sacred Sicilian strait, which in old times joined Sicily to the continent of Italy? and where vast seas on each side being excited by violent storms met together, coming from opposite directions, the land between them was overwhelmed and broken away; from which circumstance the city built in the neighborhood was called Rhegium, {rheμgion, from rhoμgnymi, "to break."} and the result was quite different from what any one would have expected; for the seas which had formerly been separated now flowed together and were united in one expanse; and the land which had previously united was now separated into two portions by the strait which intersected it, in consequence of which Sicily, which had previously formed a part of the mainland, was now compelled to be an island. XXI. And it is said that many other cities also have disappeared, having been swallowed up by the sea which overwhelmed them; since they speak of three in Peloponnesus-"Aegira and fair Bura's walls, And Helica's lofty halls, And many a once renowned town, With wreck and seaweed overgrown," As having been formerly prosperous, but now overwhelmed by the violent influx of the sea. And the island of Atalantes which was greater than Africa and Asia, as Plato says in the Timaeus, in one day and night was overwhelmed beneath the sea in consequence of an extraordinary earthquake and inundation and suddenly disappeared, becoming sea, not indeed navigable, but full of gulfs and eddies. Therefore that imaginary and fictitious diminution of the sea has no connection with the destruction or durability of the world; for in fact it appears to recede indeed from some parts, but to rise higher in others; and it would have been proper rather not to look at only one of these results but at both together, and so to form one's opinion, since in all the disputed questions which arise in human life, a wise and honest judge will not deliver his opinion before he has heard the arguments of the advocates on both sides.[125]

Oceans were not the only things to change.

> I could mention other rivers also, far inferior to the Nile in magnitude, that have effected very great changes. Among these not the least is the Achelous, which, after passing through Acarnania, empties itself into the sea opposite the islands called Echinades, and has already joined one-half of them to the continent. [49]

This one is not reliable on two counts. One is that it is Herodotus speaking of the Egyptians (see page 56), and the other is that Egyptian priests are recounting their history. Maybe they're right on this point though. Who knows?

> Thus far I have spoken on the authority of the Egyptians and their priests. They declare that from their first king to this last-mentioned monarch, the priest of Vulcan, was a period of three hundred and forty-one generations; such, at least, they say, was the number both of their kings, and of their high-priests, during this interval. Now three hundred generations of men make ten thousand years, three generations filling up the century; and the remaining forty-one generations make thirteen hundred and forty years. Thus the whole number of years is eleven thousand, three hundred and forty; in which entire space, they said, no god had ever appeared in a human form; nothing of this kind had happened either under the former or under the later Egyptian kings. The sun, however, had within this period of time, on four several occasions, moved from his wonted course, twice rising where he now sets, and twice setting where he now rises. Egypt was in no degree affected by these changes; the productions of the land, and of the river, remained the same; nor was there anything unusual either in the diseases or the deaths. [49]

There is a distinct difference between the ages of the first three hundred generations and the last forty-one, and I have my ideas about it, but I'll let you come to the same conclusion on your own. I put this in this section because the spin of the earth changed four times. Who knows if that is true?

Nations

Most of the books I got my quotes from were called "geographies," because they spoke of nations and their histories. Almost without exception, the descriptions that were given for each nation were consistent with what we know about them today. Even India was really India.[126] The exceptions are that Libya seemed to be all the north of Africa that wasn't Egypt. Ethiopia seemed to be any nation south of Egypt and Libya.

There were many things written of India. Let's start with their earliest times.

> In the earliest times, when the inhabitants of their land were still dwelling in scattered clan-villages, Dionysus came to them from the regions to the west of them with a notable army; and he traversed all India, since there was as yet no notable city which would have been able to oppose him. [...] The soldiers of Dionysus were being consumed by a pestilential sickness, this leader, who was conspicuous for his wisdom, led his army out of the plains into the hill-country; here, where cool breezes blew and the spring waters flowed pure at their very sources, the army got rid of its sickness. [...] After this he took in hand the storing of the fruits and shared this knowledge with the Indians, and he communicated to them the discovery of wine and of all the other things useful for life. Furthermore, he became the founder of notable cities by gathering the villages together in well-situated regions, and he both taught them to honour the deity and introduced laws and courts; and, in brief, since he had been the introducer of many good works he was regarded as a god and received immortal honours. [...] And after he had reigned over all India for fifty-two years he died of old age. [...] later, their sovereignty was dissolved and the cities received a democratic form of government. [...] Many years later most of the cities had received a democratic form of government, although among certain tribes the kingship endured until the time when Alexander crossed over into Asia. [38]

They also claimed that Hercules lived there as their king. Strabo wrote this of India: "Among the statements made concerning India is also the following, that it is the custom, instead of making obeisance, to offer prayers to the kings and to all who are in authority and of superior rank."[127] You win some (customs); you lose some.

We move from the supposed tribal ancestors of India to the extinct race of the Amazons. (Why we accept some stories and not others is often a mystery to me.)

> After the death of this queen, as their account continues, women of her family, succeeding to the queenship from time to time, ruled with distinction and advanced the nation of the Amazons in both power and fame. And many generations after these events, when the excellence of these women had been noised abroad through the whole inhabited world, they say that Heracles, the son of Alcmenê and Zeus, was assigned by Eurystheus the Labour of securing the girdle of Hippolytê the Amazon. Consequently he embarked on this campaign, and coming off victorious in a great battle he not only cut to pieces the army of the Amazons but also, after taking captive Hippolytê together with her girdle, completely crushed this nation. Consequently the neighbouring barbarians, despising the weakness of this people and remembering against them their past injuries, waged continuous wars against the nation to such a degree that they left in existence not even the name of the race of the Amazons. For a few years after the campaign of Heracles against them, they say, during the time of the Trojan War, Penthesileia, the queen of the surviving Amazons, who was a daughter of Ares and had slain one of her kindred, fled from her native land because of the sacrilege. And fighting as an ally of the Trojans after the death of Hector she slew many of the Greeks, and after gaining distinction in the struggle she ended her life heroically at the hands of Achilles. 6 Now they say that Penthesileia was the last of the Amazons to win distinction for bravery and that for the future the race diminished more and more and then lost all its strength; consequently in later times,

whenever any writers recount their prowess, men consider the ancient stories about the Amazons to be fictitious tales. [38]

I have no idea where the Amazons lived, but we will travel from there through Libya, for "the Ethiopians who dwell beyond Libya . . ." [45] to Ethiopia. If you believe we all came from Africa as Neanderthals, you'll love the next two quotes.

> Now the Ethiopians, as historians relate, were the first of all men and the proofs of this statement, they say, are manifest. For that they did not come into their land as immigrants from abroad but were natives of it and so justly bear the name of "autochthones" [sprung from the soil itself] is, they maintain, conceded by practically all men . . . [45]

Our forbearers even encountered these stupid primitives. Although we can't definitively prove the intelligence of a man by the shape of his skull, you can by his actions.

> The third Ptolemy also, who was passionately fond of hunting the elephants which are found in that region, sent one of his friends named Simmias to spy out the land; and he, setting out with suitable supplies, made, as the historian Agatharchides of Cnidus asserts, a thorough investigation of the nations lying along the coast. Now he says that the nation of the "insensible" Ethiopians makes no use whatsoever of drink and that their nature does not require it for the reasons given above. And as a general thing, he relates, they have no intercourse with other nations nor does the foreign appearance of people who approach their shores have any effect upon the natives, but looking at them intently they show no emotion and their expressions remain unaltered, as if there were no one present. Indeed when a man drew his sword and brandished it at them they did not turn to flight, nor, if they were subjected to insult or even to blows, would they show irritation, and the majority were not moved to anger in sympathy with the victims of such treatment; on the contrary, when at times children or women were butchered

> before their eyes they remained "insensible" in their attitudes, displaying no sign of anger or, on the other hand, of pity. In short, they remained unmoved in the face of the most appalling horrors, looking steadfastly at what was taking place and nodding their heads at each incident. Consequently, they say, they speak no language, but by movements of the hands which describe each object they point out everything they need. And the most marvellous fact of all is that seals live with these tribes and catch the fish for themselves in a manner similar to that employed by the human beings. Likewise with respect to their lairs and the safety of their offspring these two kinds of beings place the greatest faith in one another; for the association with animals of a different species continues without any wrongdoing and with peace and complete observance of propriety. Now this manner of life, strange as it is, has been observed by these tribes from very early times, whether it has been fashioned by habit over the long space of time or by a need imposed by necessity because of stress of circumstances. [38]

Now before you get too carried away and start changing the whole scientific mindset because of a couple quotes, you should be aware that there are studies that show that part of a man's aptitude is inherited by his parents.[128] Whether this is by nurture or nature, the "Insensible Ethiopians" do not show anything, one way or the other, about evolution or the flood of Noah. I just thought it was interesting, and I'm sure you will too.

Let's swim around Western Africa to the land of the Gauls.

> From this union she bore to Heracles a son named Galates, who far surpassed all the youths of the tribe in quality of spirit and strength of body. And when he had attained to man's estate and had succeeded to the throne of his fathers, he subdued a large part of the neighbouring territory and accomplished great feats in war. Becoming renowned for his bravery, he called his subjects Galatae or Gauls after himself, and these in turn gave their name to all of Galatia or Gaul. [57]

Hercules was the first king of all sorts of nations. I wonder if he gave them their wit.

> The Gauls are terrifying in aspect and their voices are deep and altogether harsh; when they meet together they converse with few words and in riddles, hinting darkly at things for the most part and using one word when they mean another; and they like to talk in superlatives, to the end that they may extol themselves and depreciate all other men. They are also boasters and threateners and are fond of pompous language, and yet they have sharp wits and are not without cleverness at learning. [57]

I've known people who do this. They usually do it as a joke, and it is entertaining.

Let's quickly move to the land of the Medes. One guy in particular was wise among a kingless tribe.

> Deioces, who was already a man of mark in his own village, applied himself with greater zeal and earnestness than ever before to the practice of justice among his fellows. […] [T]he men of his village, observing his integrity, chose him to be the arbiter of all their disputes. […]The number of complaints brought before him continually increasing […] "It did not square with his interests," he said, "to spend the whole day in regulating other men's affairs to the neglect of his own." Hereupon robbery and lawlessness broke out afresh […] Deioces […] should be king." [63]

The Medes were taken over by the Persians. Cyrus had a really interesting beginning. Did he realize that he only had the power because God was on his side? Isaiah (Chapter 44–45) names the guy hundreds of years before he was born.

> Many strong motives weighed with him and urged him on-his birth especially, which seemed something more than human, and his good fortune in all his former wars, wherein he had always found that against what country soever he turned his arms, it was impossible for that people to escape.[129]

Herodotus also talks about their customs.

> The customs which I know the Persians to observe are the following: they have no images of the gods, no temples nor altars, and consider the use of them a sign of folly. This comes, I think, from their not believing the gods to have the same nature with men, as the Greeks imagine. Their wont, however, is to ascend the summits of the loftiest mountains, and there to offer sacrifice to Jupiter, which is the name they give to the whole circuit of the firmament. They likewise offer to the sun and moon, to the earth, to fire, to water, and to the winds. These are the only gods whose worship has come down to them from ancient times. At a later period they began the worship of Urania, which they borrowed from the Arabians and Assyrians. Mylitta is the name by which the Assyrians know this goddess, whom the Arabians call Alitta, and the Persians Mitra.

Their beliefs are a lot closer to that which the Bible proclaims, though they are clearly tainted. For God, it must have been better the Persians to conquer than some other nation. In fact, they even sacrificed like Abraham.

> To these gods the Persians offer sacrifice in the following manner: they raise no altar, light no fire, pour no libations; there is no sound of the flute, no putting on of chaplets, no consecrated barley-cake; but the man who wishes to sacrifice brings his victim to a spot of ground which is pure from pollution, and there calls upon the name of the god to whom he intends to offer. It is usual to have the turban encircled with a wreath, most commonly of myrtle. The sacrificer is not allowed to pray for blessings on himself alone, but he prays for the welfare of the king, and of the whole Persian people, among whom he is of necessity included. He cuts the victim in pieces, and having boiled the flesh, he lays it out upon the tenderest herbage that he can find, trefoil especially. When all is ready, one of the Magi comes forward and chants a hymn, which they say recounts the origin of the gods. It is not lawful

to offer sacrifice unless there is a Magus present. After waiting a short time the sacrificer carries the flesh of the victim away with him, and makes whatever use of it he may please.

They had a priest help with the sacrifices. They celebrated birthdays![130] Let's end Persia's history with this lovely story about their attempt at a conquest of Ethiopia.

> Before, however, he had accomplished one-fifth part of the distance, all that the army had in the way of provisions failed; whereupon the men began to eat the sumpter beasts, which shortly failed also.... So long as the earth gave them anything, the soldiers sustained life by eating the grass and herbs; but when they came to the bare sand, a portion of them were guilty of a horrid deed: by tens they cast lots for a man, who was slain to be the food of the others. When Cambyses heard of these doings, alarmed at such cannibalism, he gave up his attack on Ethiopia, and retreating by the way he had come, reached Thebes, after he had lost vast numbers of his soldiers.[131]

I think that speaks for itself...

Let's move to the strange customs of Egypt. Herodotus thought highly of the Egyptians. It is a perception I do not entirely share.

> The Egyptians, they said, were the first to discover the solar year, and to portion out its course into twelve parts. They obtained this knowledge from the stars. The Egyptians, they went on to affirm, first brought into use the names of the twelve gods, which the Greeks adopted from them; and first erected altars, images, and temples to the gods; and also first engraved upon stone the figures of animals. In most of these cases they proved to me that what they said was true. And they told me that the first man who ruled over Egypt was Min, and that in his time all Egypt, except the Thebaic canton, was a marsh, none of the land below Lake Moeris then showing itself above the surface of the water. [49]

I tend to think that their early history is a bit tainted, as it doesn't agree with many of the other histories from other nations I've read. I wonder if he saw someone do this. "The pig is regarded among them [Egyptians] as an unclean animal, so much so that if a man in passing accidentally touch a pig, he instantly hurries to the river, and plunges in with all his clothes on." Yet, they eat them at the full moon.

> The following is the mode in which they sacrifice the swine to the Moon: As soon as the victim is slain, the tip of the tail, the spleen, and the caul are put together, and having been covered with all the fat that has been found in the animal's belly, are straightway burnt. The remainder of the flesh is eaten on the same day that the sacrifice is offered, which is the day of the full moon: at any other time they would not so much as taste it. [49]

Then he makes an inquiry of them (presumably because he was in Egypt):

> I made inquiries of the Chemmites why it was that Perseus appeared to them and not elsewhere in Egypt, and how they came to celebrate gymnastic contests unlike the rest of the Egyptians: to which they answered, "Perseus belonged to their city by descent. Danans and Lynceus were Chemmites before they set sail for Greece, and from them Perseus was descended," they said, tracing the genealogy; "and he, when he came to Egypt for the purpose" (which the Greeks also assign) "of bringing away from Libya the Gorgon's head, paid them a visit, and acknowledged them for his kinsmen- he had heard the name of their city from his mother before he left Greece- he bade them institute a gymnastic contest in his honour, and that was the reason why they observed the practice." [49]

Let me just mention here that although Chem looks like it could be rendered Shem, it could almost as easily be rendered Ham. They were not Semites (or Shemites), but Hamites.

Ancient Mysteries

There are many things that the ancients describe as being strange to them. Most of those things are strange to us as well, though some of those issues have been resolved by modern science and philosophy. I will lay out a few of the more interesting mysteries they discovered.

Let's start with the changing of the landscape of the earth. Pliny wrote about Crete. "A mountain of the island of Crete having been burst asunder by the action of an earthquake, a body was found there standing upright, forty-six cubits [approx. 70 ft (12x the normal height of a man)] in height…" [132] A seventy-foot tall skeleton is impressive, if it's true. Who knows why they called it a man? I'm not going to assume they were too stupid to figure out that it wasn't. If I assume anything, it will be that they're telling fables.

There are people who had unusual characteristics.

> Varro, speaking of persons remarkable for their strength, gives us an account of Tributanus, a celebrated gladiator, and skilled in the use of the Samnitei arms; he was a man of meagre person, but possessed of extraordinary strength. Varro makes mention of his son also, who served in the army of Pompeius Magnus. He says, that in all parts of his body, even in the arms and hands, there was a network of sinews, extending across and across. The latter of these men, having been challenged by an enemy, with a single finger of the right hand, and that unarmed, vanquished him, and then seized and dragged him to the camp.[133]

In the same book, chapters 49 and 50, he talks about accounts of men with very long life spans. Diodorus speaks of half-humans.

> Before this time it had been the custom of Minos annually to dedicate to Poseidon the fairest bull born in his herds and to sacrifice it to the god; but at the time in question there was born a bull of extraordinary beauty and he sacrificed another from among those which were inferior, where-

> upon Poseidon, becoming angry at Minos, caused his wife Pasiphaê to become enamoured of the bull. And by means of the ingenuity of Daedalus Pasiphaê had intercourse with the bull and gave birth to the Minotaur, famed in the myth. [43]

Herodotus speaks of werewolves. "[F]or both the Scythians and the Greeks who dwell in Scythia say that every Neurian once a year becomes a wolf for a few days, at the end of which time he is restored to his proper shape." [131] I don't believe in half-humans. I do believe in little people though.

> They said there had grown up among them some wild young men [...they] drew lots for five of their number to go and explore the desert parts of Libya, and try if they could not penetrate further than any had done previously. The coast of Libya along the sea which washes it to the north, throughout its entire length from Egypt to Cape Soloeis [...] The young men therefore, despatched on this errand by their comrades with a plentiful supply of water and provisions, travelled at first through the inhabited region, passing which they came to the wild beast tract, whence they finally entered upon the desert, which they proceeded to cross in a direction from east to west. After journeying for many days over a wide extent of sand, they came at last to a plain where they observed trees growing; approaching them, and seeing fruit on them, they proceeded to gather it. While they were thus engaged, there came upon them some dwarfish men, under the middle height, who seized them and carried them off. The Nasamonians could not understand a word of their language, nor had they any acquaintance with the language of the Nasamonians. They were led across extensive marshes, and finally came to a town, where all the men were of the height of their conductors, and black-complexioned. A great river flowed by the town, running from west to east, and containing crocodiles. [49]

I also believe in big people. "The people of Chemmis say that Perseus often appears to them, sometimes within the sacred enclosure, sometimes in the open country: one of the sandals which he has worn is frequently found- two cubits in length, as they affirm-" [49] Also in book three, he writes, "They [Scythians] show a footmark of Hercules, impressed on a rock, in shape like the print of a man's foot, but two cubits in length." If you don't believe his sources, then you don't believe him. Herodotus wrote, "Thus far I have spoken of Egypt from my own observation, relating what I myself saw, the ideas that I formed, and the results of my own researches."

There are also animals that were mysterious to them and even more mysterious to us. Pliny called this creature a *dragon.* [89]

> There [Libya] are also, as some say, in the country of the wild beasts, as it is called, serpents which are marvellous for their size and multitude; these attack the elephants at the water-holes, pit their strength against them, and winding themselves in coils about their legs continue squeezing them tighter and tighter in their bands until at last the beasts, covered with foam, fall to the ground from their weight. Thereupon the serpents gather and devour the flesh of the fallen elephant, overcoming the beast with ease because it moves only with difficulty. But since it still remains a puzzle why, in pursuit of their accustomed food, they do not follow the elephants into the region along the river, which I have mentioned, they say that the serpents of such great size avoid the level part of the country and continually make their homes at the foot of mountains in ravines which are suitable to their length and in deep caves; consequently they never leave the regions which are suitable to them and to which they are accustomed, Nature herself being the instructor of all the animals in such matters. [45]

He writes of more in the same chapter. In the following description, the only thing that I can think of that resembles a bull, has horns, and might eat meat is a triceratops. How those horns might be moved, though, is hard to say. They seem pretty connected to the skull. It might be a different animal entirely. You can make up your own mind.

> But of all the animals named the carnivorous bull is the wildest and altogether the hardest to overcome. For in bulk he is larger than the domestic bulls, in swiftness of foot he is not inferior to a horse, and his mouth open clear back to the ears. His colour is a fiery red, his eyes are more piercing than those of a lion and shine at night, and his horns enjoy a distinctive property; for at all other times he moves them like his ears, but when fighting he holds them rigid. The direction of growth of his hair is contrary to that of all other animals. He is, again, a remarkable beast in both boldness and strength, since he attacks the boldest animals and finds his food in devouring the flesh of his victims. He also destroys the flocks of the inhabitants and engages in terrible combats with whole bands of the shepherds and packs of dogs. Rumour has it that their skin cannot be pierced; at any rate, though many men have tried to capture them, no man has ever brought one under subjection. If he has fallen into a pit or been captured by some other ruse he becomes choked with rage, and in no case does he ever exchange his freedom for the care which men would accord to him in domestication. It is with reason, therefore, that the Trogodytes hold this wild beast to be the strongest of all, since Nature has endowed it with the prowess of a lion, the speed of a horse, and the might of a bull, and since it is not subdued by the native strength of iron which is the greatest known.

Herodotus also speaks of griffins. "[T]he Samians made a brazen vessel, in shape like an Argive wine-bowl, adorned with the heads of griffins standing out in high relief." [131] Hyginus recounts the history behind using a wreath of parsley.

> The seven chieftains on their way to attack Thebes came to Nemea, where Hypsipyle, daughter of Thoas, as a slave, was caring for the boy Archemorus or Ophites, son of King Lycus. He had been warned by an oracle not to put the child on the ground until he could walk. When the seven leaders who were going to Thebes came to Hypsipyle in their search for water, and asked her to show them some, she, fearing to put the boy on the ground, ... [found] some very

> thick parsley near the spring, and placed the child in it. But while she was giving them water, a dragon, guardian of the spring, devoured the child. Adrastus and the others killed the dragon, and interceded for Hypsipyle to Lycus, and established funeral games in honour of the boy. They take place every fifth year, and the victors receive a wreath of parsley.

Poor kid. I think he should have realized that dragons don't exist. There are also pterodactyls that have been observed. "[A]nd that in other places there are reptiles two cubits long with membranous wings like bats, and that they too fly by night, discharging drops of urine, or also of sweat, which putrefy the skin of anyone who is not on his guard…" [127] Herodotus speaks of flying snakes. I wonder if they are the same thing. "The winged serpent is shaped like the water-snake. Its wings are not feathered, but resemble very closely those of the bat." [49]

There were signs in the heavens. "[J]ust as the battle was growing warm, day was on a sudden changed into night." [63] This resembles that event the Egyptians spoke of, with the sun changing direction four times in history.

Some speculations were since solved by modern investigation.

> [T]he priests of Egypt assert that the Nile has its origin in the ocean which surrounds the inhabited world, there is nothing sound in what they say, and they are merely solving one perplexity by substituting another, and advancing as proof an explanation which itself stands much in need of proof. [53]

They guessed right on the shape of the globe. "[E]specially if one holds to the theory that the earth is shaped like a sphere." [53]

Be careful whom you attack.

> The Scythians who plundered the temple were punished by the goddess with the female sickness, which still attaches to their posterity. They themselves confess that they are afflicted with the disease for this reason, and travellers who visit Scythia can see what sort of a disease it is. Those who suffer from it are called Enarees. [6]

I wonder who plundered the temple. Stupid people. Then again, maybe it was the people who attributed this disease to the plundering of a temple that were stupid. I don't really know. Maybe I'm stupid. You're no better! Where's your authority for the position you took?

Finally, the Scythians. They were an antisocial bunch.

> There the body of the dead [Scythian] king is laid in the grave prepared for it, stretched upon a mattress; spears are fixed in the ground on either side of the corpse, and beams stretched across above it to form a roof, which is covered with a thatching of osier twigs. In the open space around the body of the king they bury one of his concubines, first killing her by strangling, and also his cup-bearer, his cook, his groom, his lacquey, his messenger, some of his horses, firstlings of all his other possessions, and some golden cups; for they use neither silver nor brass.
> When a year is gone by, further ceremonies take place. Fifty of the best of the late king's attendants are taken, all native Scythians- for, as bought slaves are unknown in the country, the Scythian kings choose any of their subjects that they like, to wait on them- fifty of these are taken and strangled, with fifty of the most beautiful horses. When they are dead.

That is very sad, indeed. We can learn a few things from them about what not to do in life. They also throw hemp on a fire and don't take a bath:

> The Scythians, as I said, take some of this hemp-seed, and, creeping under the felt coverings, throw it upon the red-hot stones; immediately it smokes, and gives out such a vapour as no Grecian vapour-bath can exceed; the Scyths, delighted, shout for joy, and this vapour serves them instead of a water-bath ...[131]

I've known people like that. I suppose if you smell of burnt hemp, you don't need a bath.

Random Finds

I got myself into a witty mood by talking about female diseases and hemp, so let's start looking at some of the funny, interesting, and strange things these historians thought were right to put in their work.

Diodorus decided to mock the mustache.

> Some of them shave the beard, but others let it grow a little; and the nobles shave their cheeks, but they let the moustache grow until it covers the mouth. Consequently, when they are eating, their moustaches become entangled in the food, and when they are drinking, the beverage passes, as it were, through a kind of a strainer. [57]

From the humorous, we move to the disgusting.

> The wives of men of rank are not given to be embalmed immediately after death, nor indeed are any of the more beautiful and valued women. It is not till they have been dead three or four days that they are carried to the embalmers. This is done to prevent indignities from being offered them. It is said that once a case of this kind occurred: the man was detected by the information of his fellow-workman. [49]

The Egyptians were not the only ones who were sexually perverse. This king had problems, in more than one way.

> Now it happened that this Candaules was in love with his own wife; and not only so, but thought her the fairest woman in the whole world. This fancy had strange consequences. There was in his bodyguard a man whom he specially favoured, Gyges, the son of Dascylus. All affairs of greatest moment were entrusted by Candaules to this person, and to him he was wont to extol the surpassing beauty of his wife. So matters went on for a while. At length, one day, Candaules, who was fated to end ill, thus addressed his follower: "I see thou dost not credit what I tell thee of my lady's loveliness;

but come now, since men's ears are less credulous than their eyes, contrive some means whereby thou mayst behold her naked." At this the other loudly exclaimed, saying, "What most unwise speech is this, master, which thou hast uttered? […]" […] But the king replied to him, "Courage, friend; suspect me not of the design to prove thee by this discourse; nor dread thy mistress, lest mischief be thee at her hands. Be sure I will so manage that she shall not even know that thou hast looked upon her. I will place thee behind the open door of the chamber in which we sleep. When I enter to go to rest she will follow me. There stands a chair close to the entrance, on which she will lay her clothes one by one as she takes them off. Thou wilt be able thus at thy leisure to peruse her person. Then, when she is moving from the chair toward the bed, and her back is turned on thee, be it thy care that she see thee not as thou passest through the doorway." Gyges, unable to escape, could but declare his readiness. Then Candaules, when bedtime came, led Gyges into his sleeping-chamber, and a moment after the queen followed. She entered, and laid her garments on the chair, and Gyges gazed on her. After a while she moved toward the bed, and her back being then turned, he glided stealthily from the apartment. As he was passing out, however, she saw him, and instantly divining what had happened, she neither screamed as her shame impelled her, nor even appeared to have noticed aught, purposing to take vengeance upon the husband who had so affronted her. [… she] summoned Gyges into her presence. […] He […] obeyed the summons, not suspecting that she knew aught of what had occurred. Then she addressed these words to him: "Take thy choice, Gyges, of two courses which are open to thee. Slay Candaules, and thereby become my lord, and obtain the Lydian throne, or die this moment in his room. […] he made choice of life for himself […] She placed a dagger in his hand and hid him carefully behind the self-same door. Then Gyges, when the king was fallen asleep, entered privily into the chamber and struck him dead. [63]

Boy, that was fun. It almost seems like shame for nakedness is becoming a thing of the past. It was better when people faced death for peeping.

My last story has to do with another king's vanity. We really should be more humble.

> On this account, as well as to see the world, Solon set out upon his travels, in the course of which he went to Egypt to the court of Amasis, and also came on a visit to Croesus at Sardis. Croesus received him as his guest, and lodged him in the royal palace. On the third or fourth day after, he bade his servants conduct Solon over his treasuries, and show him all their greatness and magnificence. When he had seen them all, and, so far as time allowed, inspected them, Croesus addressed this question to him. "Stranger of Athens, we have heard much of thy wisdom and of thy travels through many lands, from love of knowledge and a wish to see the world. I am curious therefore to inquire of thee, whom, of all the men that thou hast seen, thou deemest the most happy?" This he asked because he thought himself the happiest of mortals: but Solon answered him without flattery, according to his true sentiments, "Tellus of Athens, sire." Full of astonishment at what he heard, Croesus demanded sharply, "And wherefore dost thou deem Tellus happiest?" To which the other replied, "First, because his country was flourishing in his days, and he himself had sons both beautiful and good, and he lived to see children born to each of them, and these children all grew up; and further because, after a life spent in what our people look upon as comfort, his end was surpassingly glorious. In a battle between the Athenians and their neighbours near Eleusis, he came to the assistance of his countrymen, routed the foe, and died upon the field most gallantly. The Athenians gave him a public funeral on the spot where he fell, and paid him the highest honours." [63]

Croesus insults him again by saying that there were two others who had been honored at the Olympic Games that were happier. Solon asked, incredulous, what that makes him.

> "For assuredly he who possesses great store of riches is no nearer happiness than he who has what suffices for his daily needs, unless it so hap that luck attend upon him, and so he continue in the enjoyment of all his good things to the end of life."

This is a powerful statement, "[N]o single human being is complete in every respect—something is always lacking."

In the end, Croesus lost his son, and he wasn't very happy. The moral of this story is that there aren't always morals to the story. This is a heap of garbage. I have seen people who were happy throughout their lives. They didn't care a lick about the honor bestowed by men. They gained and lost throughout, but the thing that brought them happiness was that they had the true hope of eternity, and they were living for someone other than themselves.

Thus ends my appendix and my book. I hope you have enjoyed it, and perhaps, if I'm lucky, I will have done you the service of making you better by it. If you have any questions, please feel free to ask. Count me your servant. Nothing would make me happier.

BOOK REFERENCES

If you want to do further study in any areas that I talked about in this book, I highly recommend that you do. I lay out the sources in one place so that you can more easily find them later. The sources are ordered by usefulness:

Bill Cooper, *After the Flood,* a book showing we all descend from Noah

http://ldolphin.org/cooper/index.html

Bill Cooper, *The Table of Nations,* shows where Noah's descendants went

http://www.biblebelievers.org.au/natindx.htm#Index

Arthur C. Custance, *Noah's Three Sons,* shows where Noah's descendants went

http://custance.org/old/noah/index.html

Ian Taylor, *In the Minds of Men,* a book on the history of the Theory of Evolution

http://www.creationism.org/books/TaylorInMindsMen/index.htm

Do-While Jones, Science Against Evolution Newsletter, Evolution cannot be true

http://www.scienceagainstevolution.org/topics.htm

Richard Lynche, *Travels of Noah into Europe* (1601, London)

http://www.argyrou.eclipse.co.uk/myths/bible/Travels.htm

Mythology Made Easy

http://www.annomundi.com/history/mythology_made_easy.htm

Kent Hovind (Dr. Dino), videos, shows the absurdity of evolution and the usefulness of the Bible

http://www.arrivalofthefittest.com/csehovind.html

Walter Brown, *In the Beginning,* a theory about the flood

http://creationscience.com/onlinebook/

Convergent Evolution, how many times can we get the same thing independently?

http://en.wikipedia.org/wiki/List_of_examples_of_convergent_evolution

Eusebius, *Chronicle* (263–339 AD, Caesarea / Israel)

http://www.attalus.org/translate/eusebius4.html

Josephus, *Antiquities of the Jews* (37–100 AD, Jerusalem / Israel)

http://www.sacred-texts.com/jud/josephus/ant-1.htm

Diodorus Siculus, *The Library of History* (~50 BC, Sicily)

http://penelope.uchicago.edu/Thayer/E/Roman/Texts/Diodorus_Siculus/

Strabo, *The Geography* (63/64 BC–24 AD, Rome)

http://penelope.uchicago.edu/Thayer/E/Roman/Texts/Strabo/

Herodotus, *The History of Herodotus* (484–425 BC, Greece)

http://classics.mit.edu/Herodotus/history.mb.txt

Pliny the Elder, *The Natural History* (23–79 AD, Rome)

http://www.perseus.tufts.edu/hopper/text;?doc=Perseus%3atext%3a1999.02.0137

Dionysius of Halicarnassus, *Roman Antiquities* (60–7 BC, Rome)

http://penelope.uchicago.edu/Thayer/E/Roman/Texts/Dionysius_of_Halicarnassus/home.html

My site, the text of this book, with updated and clickable links

http://www.fromnoahtohercules.com/

ENDNOTES

1 Dolphin, Lambert. "World Population Since Creation." Originally written 1987, last update July 31, 2007.http://ldolphin.org/popul.html (accessed July 15, 2010).

2 Wikipedia, "Age of the universe." July 14, 2010. http://en.wikipedia.org/wiki/Age_of_the_universe (accessed July 15, 2010). Much of this was taken from here. See note 9 on the use of Wikipedia as a source in this book.

3 If evolution is true, atheism is too. Here is how I would get from Adam to atheism: God set up death. Adam did not bring it into being. Death is not a result of our sin. We are being punished without ever having sinned. We do not need salvation. On the contrary, we need to be saved from God, if he/she even exists. This whole scenario of Adam is illogical. It is a story told to ancient Hebrew children in order to keep them in line. That would be the train that would lead me to atheism.

4 Let me state here that, in my experience, the Darwinist's complaint of ignorance about Creationists is very appropriate. Nobody in my circle of friends knew enough to help me through this problem. I thank God that there are those out there who have studied this topic and who helped me find wisdom.

5 "Kent Hovind Videos." http://www.arrivalofthefittest.com/csehovind.html (accessed July 15, 2010).

6 Taylor, Ian. *In the Minds of Men.* 5th ed. Zimmerman, MN: TFE Publishing, 1984, 1987, 1991, 1999, 2003.

7 Cooper, Bill. *After the Flood.* Internet ed. West Sussex Po20 6YB, England: New Wine Press, 1995.

8 Lynche, Richard. *AN HISTORICAL TREATISE OF THE TRAVELS OF NOAH INTO Europe : Containing the first inhabita- tion and peopling thereof.* London: Adam Islip, 1601. http://www.argyrou.eclipse.co.uk/myths/bible/Travels.htm (accessed July 15, 2010).

9 Note on sources used in this book (particularly this chapter): You will notice that throughout this book I use Wikipedia.org as a source. I have not used them because I put a lot of stock in the opinions expressed there. On the contrary! Excepting the cases where it is obvious why, I used them to show what opinions are being expressed in popular culture. Each article is supposed to be linked to real sources, so you can feel free to follow the claims to "real proof" from there. A few other sources might not be considered reliable by everyone. If you don't think the source I used is trustworthy, don't trust it. Missing a few of my sources won't collapse my argument. If you don't like my source, ignore the point and move on!

10 Matthew 1, Luke 3

11 "Man (is) appointed mortal sorrow; (but) the Blessed God shall come down teaching (that) His death shall bring (the) despairing rest."Missler, Chuck. "The Gospel in Genesis." http://www.khouse.org/articles/1996/44/ (accessed July 15, 2010).

12 The Romulans of Star Trek, not the descendants of Romulus (or the Romans), though they probably could too!

13 "Time itself passes more quickly when gravity is reduced." Ritter, Malcom. "Ultra-precise atomic clocks will redefine time." 9/10/2006. http://www.msnbc.msn.com/id/14739827/ (accessed July 15, 2010).

14 Chui, Christopher. http://www.darwinisdead.com/archive/9_19_09%20Christopher_Chui.wmv (accessed July 15, 2010).

15 Wikipedia, "List of examples of convergent evolution." May 6, 2010. http://en.wikipedia.org/wiki/List_of_examples_of_convergent_evolution (accessed July 15, 2010).

16 Woodmorappe, John. "Walking whales, nested hierarchies, and chimeras: do they exist?." April, 2002. http://www.answersingenesis.org/tj/v16/i1/chimeras.asp (accessed July 15, 2010).

17 Similar: Jones, Do-While. "Biogeography." Sept. 2009. http://www.scienceagainstevolution.org/v13i12f.htm (accessed July 15, 2010).

18 Wikipedia, "Radiometric dating." June 1, 2010. http://en.wikipedia.org/wiki/Radiometric_dating (accessed July 15, 2010).

19 ICR "Radioisotopes and the Age of the Earth (RATE)." http://www.icr.org/rate/ (accessed July 15, 2010)

20 Hoesch, Bill. http://www.darwinisdead.com/archive/2_6_10%20Bill_Hoesch.wmv (accessed July 15, 2010) <- This one is really good.

21 Jones, Do-While. "Exact Dating (More or Less)." Feb. 1997. http://www.scienceagainstevolution.org/v1i5f.htm (accessed July 15, 2010).

22 Berg, Randy S. . "Radiometric Dating and the Age of the Earth." 2006. http://www.earthage.org/EarthOldorYoung/Radiometric Dating, and The Age of the Earth.htm (accessed July 15, 2010).

23 "In *The Genesis Flood,* I had heard that paraconformity was a word used by evolutionary geologists for fossil systems out of order, but with no evidence of erosion or overthrusting. My heart really started pounding when paraconformities and other unconformities came up in geology class. What did the professor say? Essentially the same thing as Morris and Whitcomb. He presented paraconformities as a real mystery and something very difficult to explain in evolutionary or uniformitarian terms." Parker, Gary. "From Evolution to Creation: A Personal Testimony." http://www.icr.org/articles/view/95/ (accessed July 15, 2010).

24 Brown, Walt. *In the Beginning: Compelling Evidence for Creation and the Flood.* 8th ed. Center for Scientific Creation, 1995–2008. - The entire book is useful for evi-

dence and speculation about how to interpret the geological record.

25 "We don't have all the explanations as to how the evidence came to be that way, and it may be that in the future we will discover some human fossils. However, there is also much about the fossil record that the evolutionists have a hard time explaining. On the other hand, we should also realize that we don't have all the answers either, and we never will." Snelling, Andrew A. . "Where are all the human fossils?." 1991. http://www.answersingenesis.org/creation/v14/i1/humanfossils.asp (accessed July 15, 2010).

26 Weston, William. "La Brea Tar Pits: Evidence of a Catastrophic Flood." June 2003. http://www.creationresearch.org/crsq/articles/40/40_1/LaBrea3.htm (accessed July 15, 2010). Read at: Diluvial Sorting and the Geologic Periods

27 "... I observed that there were shells upon the hills ..."–Herodotus, book 2 (See note 49.)

28 "We observed that, in our own times, fish had been found on top of the highest peaks of the Libanus mountains ..."–Eusebius, Hebrews (see note 100)

29 EnchantedLearning.com, "HOW FOSSILS FORM." 1996–2010. http://www.enchantedlearning.com/subjects/dinosaurs/dinofossils/Fossilhow.html (accessed July 15, 2010).

30 creationwiki.org, "Stalactite and stalagmite." June 2010. http://creationwiki.org/Stalactite_and_stalagmite (accessed July 15, 2010). When I'm at the beach, I take a handful of wet sand and let it drip through. I repeat this process. After only a minute or two, the mound of wet sand has turned to a mound of damp sand, far more stable than it was only a minute before. Observing this process helps me to see that it's not only possible that a stalagmite would form quickly, but it's likely.

31 http://www.culturedlabdiamonds.com/ - Man made diamonds for sale.

32 Balogh, Rick. “Does Fossilization Require Millions of Years?.” http://www.creationinthecrossfire.com/Articles/Fossilization.htm (accessed July 15, 2010).

33 “’Petrified’ Objects in Two Weeks!” http://creationtruthministries.org/storenews.html (accessed July 15, 2010). You can buy a manufactured petrified rose or teddy bear.

34 I recommend these videos featuring Dr. David Menton: Fearfully & Wonderfully Made, The Hearing Ear and the Seeing Eye, and Formed to Fly.

35 I came to this conclusion without help, as it’s obvious to a thinker, but I ran across this quote just recently. It is an old argument. ‘Epicurus […] saw that if those atoms of his were always falling downwards by their own weight, their motion would be fixed and predetermined, and there would be no room for free will in the world. So casting about for a way to avoid this determinism, which Democritus had apparently overlooked, he said that the atoms, as they fell, just swerved a little!’ Cooper, Bill. *After the Flood.* Internet ed. Chapter 1. West Sussex Po20 6YB, England: New Wine Press, 1995.

36 Diodorus Siculus. *The Library of History.* Book 1, 50 BC “Now as for the stories invented by Herodotus and certain writers on Egyptian affairs, who deliberately preferred to the truth the telling of marvellous tales and the invention of myths for the delectation of their readers, these we shall omit, and we shall set forth only what appears in the written records of the priests of Egypt and has passed our careful scrutiny.”

37 Strabo, *The Geography,* book 1,Approx. 10 BC

38 Diodorus Siculus. *The Library of History.* Book 2, 50 BC.

39 Custance, Arthur C. . *Noah’s Three Sons.* Online ed. Evelyn White. Lambert Dolphin, December 16, 1996.

40 Cooper, Bill. “The Table of Nations.” http://www.biblebelievers.org.au/natindx.htm#Index (accessed July 15, 2010).

41 Augustine wrote, "But was that Euhemerus also a poet, who declares both Jupiter himself, and his father Saturn, and Pluto and Neptune his brothers, to have been men, in terms so exceedingly plain that their worshippers ought all the more to render thanks to the poets, because their inventions have not been intended so much to disparage them as rather to dress them up? Albeit Cicero mentions that this same Euhemerus was translated into Latin by the poet Ennius. Or was Cicero himself a poet, who, in counselling the person with whom he debates in his Tusculan Disputations, addresses him as one possessing knowledge of things secret, in the following terms: If, indeed, I were to attempt to search into antiquity, and produce from thence the subjects which the writers of Greece have given to the world, it would be found that even those deities who are reckoned gods of the higher orders have gone from us into heaven. Ask whose sepulchres are pointed out in Greece: call to mind, since you have been initiated, the things which are delivered in the mysteries: then, doubtless, you will comprehend how widely extended this belief is. *This author certainly makes ample acknowledgment of the doctrine that those gods of theirs were originally men.* He does, indeed, benevolently surmise that they made their way into heaven. But he did not hesitate to say in public, that even the honour thus given them in general repute was conferred upon them by men, when he spoke of Romulus in these words: By good will and repute we have raised to the immortal gods that Romulus who founded this city. How should it be such a wonderful thing, therefore, to suppose that the more ancient men did with respect to Jupiter and Saturn and the others what the Romans have done with respect to Romulus, and what, in good truth, they have thought of doing even in these more recent times also in the case of Cæsar?" Augustine, "The Harmony of the Gospels, Book 1." http://www.newadvent.org/fathers/1602123.htm (accessed July 15, 2010). Emphasis mine.

42 Strabo, *The Geography*, book 2, Approx. 10 BC

43 Diodorus Siculus. *The Library of History.* Book 4, 50 BC.

44 Strabo, book 2 (see note 42); Note: Pygmies do exist. He doubted too strongly. I've seen long-headed skulls.

45 Diodorus Siculus. *The Library of History.* Book 3, 50 BC.

46 Pliny the Elder. *The Natural History.* Book 7, chapter 37. Approx. 50 AD.

47 Pliny the Elder. *The Natural History.* Book 7, chapter 30. Approx. 50 AD.

48 Diodorus, book 1 (see note 53), also Strabo writes in his first book (see note 37): "The scene is small when the activities are of small importance, and large when they are of large importance; and the largest is the scene that embraces all the rest (which we call by the special name of 'the inhabited world') and this, therefore, would be the scene of activities of the largest importance." In other words, the more people and regions are affected, the more important.

49 Herodotus. *The History of Herodotus.* Book 2. 450 BC.

50 Strabo wrote in book 2 (see note 42): "For they are the persons who tell us about the 'men that sleep in their ears,' and the 'men without mouths,' and 'men without noses'; and about 'men with one eye,' 'men with long legs,' 'men with fingers turned backward'; and they revived, also, the Homeric story of the battle between the cranes and the 'pygmies,' who, they say, were three spans tall. These men also tell about the ants that mine gold and Pans with wedge-shaped heads; and about snakes that swallow oxen and stags, horns and all; and in these matters the one refutes the other, as is stated by Eratosthenes also."–Three spans is about 27 inches or 70 cm.

51 Strabo, *The Geography*, book 3, Approx. 10 BC, he measures the earth from England to India, from the North to "Etheopia", mentioning the temperate zones on either side of the equator. Pliny the Elder. *The Natural History.*

Book 2, chapter 68. Approx. 50 AD., "For the globe is divided into five parts, termed zones, and all that portion is subject to severe cold and perpetual frost which is under the two extremities, about each of the poles, the nearer of which is called the north, and the opposite the south, pole. In all these regions there is perpetual darkness, and, in consequence of the aspect of the milder stars being turned from them, the light is malignant, and only like the whiteness which is produced by hoar frost. The middle of the earth, over which is the orbit of the sun, is parched and burned by the flame, and is consumed by being so near the heat. There are only two of the zones which are temperate, those which lie between the torrid and the frigid zones, and these are separated from each other, in consequence of the scorching heat of the heavenly bodies."

52 Philo, *On the Creation.* Online ed. Cornerstone Publications, Approx 30 AD.

53 Diodorus Siculus. *The Library of History.* Book 1, 50 BC.

54 Hyginus, *Fabulae,* #142 Pandora, Approx 50 AD.

55 Hyginus, *Fabulae,* #154 Phaethon of Hesiod, Approx 50 AD.

56 Hyginus, *Fabulae,* #152 A. Phaethon & 153 Deucalion and Pyrrha, Approx. 50 AD.

57 Diodorus Siculus. *The Library of History.* Book 5, 50 BC

58 Josephus, *Antiquities of the Jews,* Book 1: *Creation to Death of Isaac.,* Chap. 8, Approx. 70 AD.: "He [Abraham] communicated to them [the learned Egyptians] arithmetic, and delivered to them the science of astronomy; for before Abram came into Egypt they were unacquainted with those parts of learning; for that science came from the Chaldeans into Egypt, and from thence to the Greeks also."

59 Diodorus Siculus. *The Library of History.* Book 6, 50 BC

60 Philo, *Concerning the World.* Online ed. Cornerstone Publications, Approx 30 AD.

61 Be cautious of ancient dates. Some are exaggerated. Some are miscalculated. Some are made up. For instance, the Egyptians reckoned a year as 30 days. "Consequently, since the year consisted of thirty days, it was not impossible that some men lived twelve hundred years…" (Diodorus, book 1, see note 53) And if months were reckoned as years, 17,000 months would mean approx. 1,400 years.

62 Philo, *Concerning Noah's work as a Planter.* Online ed. Cornerstone Publications, Approx 30 AD.

63 Herodotus. *The History of Herodotus.* Book 1. 450 BC.

64 Dionysius of Halicarnassus, R*oman Antiquities.* Book 1, Approx 20 BC.

65 "Now as for the stories invented by Herodotus and certain writers on Egyptian affairs…"–Diodorus, book 1 (See note 53)

66 Don't take my word for it; I find the thing a mystery. Eusebius wrote, "But Manetho, who was by birth an Egyptian, had some knowledge of Greek learning, as is very evident; for he wrote the history of his own country in the Greek language, by translating it, as he says himself, out of their sacred records; he also finds great fault with Herodotus for his ignorance and inaccuracy about Egyptian history." Eusebius, *Chronicle. The Hebrews.* Approx 330 AD.

67 Catholic.com, Annius of Viterbo. http://oce.catholic.com/index.php?title=Annius_of_Viterbo (accessed July 15, 2010).

68 Gascoigne, Mike. *Forgotten History of the Western People.* Anno Mundi Books, October 24, 2002.

69 Lynche, Richard. http://www.annomundi.com/history/travels_of_noah.htm (accessed July 15, 2010).

70 http://www.fromnoahtohercules.com/tne/ - TNE transcribed by me (see note 8).

71 Argyros George Argyrou, http://www.argyrou.eclipse.co.uk/myths/bible/Travels.htm (accessed July 15, 2010).

72 Gascoigne, Mike. "Mythology Made Easy." http://www.annomundi.com/history/mythology_made_easy.htm (accessed July 15, 2010).

73 Virgil translates the name as Dionysus, but this doesn't seem quite as reliable. See my appendix, page 141.

74 Nelson, Garry. "Human Giants." http://hubpages.com/hub/Human-Giants (accessed July 15, 2010).

75 Wikipedia, "Pygmy peoples." July, 2010. http://en.wikipedia.org/wiki/Pygmies (accessed July 15, 2010).

76 Jubilees 8:18 "And Noah rejoiced that this portion came forth for Shem and for his sons ..."

77 Jasher 16:11–12, *Hebrews* 5–7

78 "... they entermed him by the name Cham Esenuus, which signified their infamous god Pan." (TNE, see note 71)

79 Heinrich Schliemann discovered Troy in the late 1860's.

80 "Boccace sayth, That he [Osyris] was called also Serapis, and that the ancient Poets termed him likewise Dionysus, Liber Pater, and Bacchus ..." (TNE, see note 71)

81 Diodorus, book 1 (see note 53): "When Osiris was ruling over Egypt as its lawful king, he was murdered by his brother Typhon, a violent and impious man ..." "But Isis, the sister and wife of Osiris, avenged his murder with the aid of her son Horus, and after slaying Typhon and his accomplices became queen over Egypt." Also, "But it is generally agreed that when [giants] stirred up war against Zeus and Osiris they were all destroyed."

82 "... Gaul was first inhabited and peopled in the hundred and eight year after the general flood ..." (TNE, see note 71)

83 Jupiter was a title, not a name. "[A]nd Iupiter was such, as in Egypt Pharaoh, and Rome Caesar, and as now

their Pope: for Iupiter is as much as, Iuvaus pater : and Papa, Pater patrium." (TNE, see note 71)

84 Charles, R. H. . "The Book of Jubilees." http://www.sacred-texts.com/bib/jub/index.htm (accessed July 15, 2010).

85 "The Book of Jasher." http://www.sacred-texts.com/chr/apo/jasher/index.htm (accessed July 15, 2010).

86 Trimm, James. *The Clear Truth about the Book of* Jasher. Lulu.com, January 6, 2010., also Baskette, John. "The Book of Jasher." 1994, 2003.http://answers.org/bible/jasher-book-of.html (accessed July 15, 2010)., and Jasher.com, "JASHER NEWS & VIEWS." http://www.jasher.com/Forum.htm (accessed July 15, 2010).

87 Cromie, William J. . "Physicists Slow Speed of Light." 1999. http://www.news.harvard.edu/gazette/1999/02.18/light.html (accessed July 15, 2010).

88 Rincon, Paul. "Ice deposits found at Moon's pole." March 2, 2010. http://news.bbc.co.uk/2/hi/science/nature/8544635.stm (accessed July 15, 2010).

89 Pliny the Elder, *The Natural History.* Book 8, Chapters 11–13, 22, and 30, *THE NATURE OF THE TERRESTRIAL ANIMALS.* Approx. 60 AD. In these chapters, among other normal animals you see today, he talks about dragons, unicorns, and sphinxes. Here is a sample from chapter 22. It's clearly not a snake, which would be the closest that we have in the modern day. "When a boy, he had become much attached to it, and had reared it very tenderly; but his father, being alarmed at the nature and monstrous size of the reptile, had taken and left it in the desert. Thoas being here attacked by some robbers who lay in ambush, he was delivered from them by the dragon, which recognized his voice and came to his assistance."

90 Beowulf, chapter 11 says, "Straightway [Grendel] seized a sleeping warrior for the first, and tore him fiercely asunder, the bone-frame bit, drank blood in streams, swallowed him piecemeal: swiftly thus the lifeless corse

was clear devoured, e'en feet and hands." Ch. 12 says, "... no keenest blade, no farest of falchions fashioned on earth, could harm or hurt that hideous fiend! [...]The outlaw dire took mortal hurt; a mighty wound showed on his shoulder, and sinews cracked, and the bone-frame burst. To Beowulf now the glory was given..." This describes a beast that is like nothing we have alive in nature. A really good discussion of the text is found in Bill Cooper's book, *After the Flood,* Chapters 10–11 (see note 7).

91 Dye, Willie. http://www.darwinisdead.com/archive/9_6_08%20Willie%20Dye.wmv (accessed July 15, 2010).

92 Swift, Dennis. *Secrets of the Ica Stones and Nazca Lines.* 2006.

93 Parker, Gary. "Variation within created kinds." http://www.answersingenesis.org/home/area/cfol/ch2-variation.asp (accessed July 15, 2010).

94 This comes out of the hydroplate theory (see note 24).

95 Wikipedia, "Yonaguni Monument." July 10, 2010. http://en.wikipedia.org/wiki/Yonaguni_Monument (accessed July 15, 2010). I recently discovered a good book on this topic: Nienhuis, James I. *Ice Age Civilizations.* Genesis Veracity, 2006.

96 Deut 28:58 "If you refuse to obey all the terms of this law that are written in this book, and if you do not fear the glorious and awesome name of the Lord your God, then the Lord will overwhelm both you and your children with indescribable plagues. These plagues will be intense and without relief, making you miserable and unbearably sick. He will bring against you all the diseases of Egypt that you feared so much, and they will claim you."

97 Dionysius wrote: "For neither the Crotoniats," says Herodotus, "nor the Placians agree in language with any of their present neighbours, although they agree with each other; and it is clear that they preserve the fashion of speech which they brought with them into

those regions." However, one may well marvel that, although the Crotoniats had a speech similar to that of the Placians, who lived near the Hellespont,87 since both were originally Pelasgians, it was not at all similar to that of the Tyrrhenians, their nearest neighbours. For if kinship is to be regarded as the reason why two nations speak the same language, the contrary must, of course, be the reason for their speaking a different one, 4 since surely it is not possible to believe that both these conditions arise from the same cause. For, although it might reasonably happen, on the one hand, that men of the same nation who have settled at a distance from one another would, as the result of associating with their neighbours, no longer preserve the same fashion of speech, yet it is not at all reasonable that men sprung from the same race and living in the same country should not in the least agree with one another in their language." Dionysius of Halicarnassus, R*oman Antiquities.* Book 1, Approx 20 BC.

98 Jubilees 17:33 "And in the twenty-fifth jubilee Noah took to himself a wife, and her name was 'mzârâ, the daughter of Râkê'êl, the daughter of his father's brother, in the first year in the fifth week: and in the third year thereof she bare him Shem, in the fifth year thereof she bare him Ham, and in the first year in the sixth week she bare him Japheth."

99 Josephus, "Antiquities of the Jews." Approx. 70 AD. http://www.sacred-texts.com/jud/josephus/ant-1.htm (accessed July 15, 2010).

100 Eusebius, *Chronicle. The Hebrews.* Approx 330 AD.

101 The KJV Old Testament Hebrew Lexicon, "adam." http://www.biblestudytools.com/lexicons/hebrew/kjv/adam-2.html (accessed July 15, 2010).

102 A promising find was announced during the editing of this book. We shall see how this discovery pans out as more skeptical observers are able to view it. http://www.noahsarksearch.net/eng/

103 *Noah's Three Sons,* Arthur C. Custance; *The Table of Nations,* Bill Cooper

104 Proof is here: Clement, "The Recognitions of Clement." http://www.compassionatespirit.com/Recognitions/Book-4.htm (accessed July 15, 2010)., Jasher 7:23–9:39 (9:21 especially)

105 "... Italy, which was then called Saturnia." (Dionysius of Halicarnassus, see note 64)

106 Dionysius also states this about Italy (see note 64): "But whether, as Antiochus says, the country took this name from a ruler, which perhaps is more probable, or, as Hellanicus believes, from the bull, yet this at least is evident from both their accounts, that in Hercules' time, or a little earlier, it received this name. Before that it had been called Hesperia and Ausonia by the Greeks and Saturnia by the natives, as I have already stated." And "There is another legend related by the inhabitants, to the effect that before the reign of Jupiter Saturn was lord in this land and that the celebrated manner of life in his reign, abounding in the produce of every season, was enjoyed by none more than them." "It is no wonder, therefore, that the ancients looked upon this country as sacred to Saturn, since they esteemed this god to be the giver and accomplisher of all happiness to mankind,—whether he ought to be called Cronus, as the Greeks deem fitting, or Saturn, as do the Romans,—and regarded him as embracing the whole universe, by whichever name he is called, and since they saw this country abounding in universal plenty and every charm mankind craves, and judged those places to be most agreeable both to divine and to human beings that are suited to them ..."

107 Proverbs 18:13. Even if you're like my wife, who is only curious, not a fool, go back to read the rest first. So much of what I say here depends on what I've said before.

108 Descartes wrote in his *Meditations* (approx 1640): "Their source is the fact that my will has a wider scope than my intellect has, ·so that I am free to form beliefs on topics

that I don't understand·. Instead of ·behaving as I ought to, namely by· restricting my will to the territory that my understanding covers, ·that is, suspending judgment when I am not intellectually in control·, I let my will run loose, applying it to matters that I don't understand. In such cases there is nothing to stop the will from veering this way or that, so it easily turns away from what is true and good. That is the source of my error and sin."

109 Matthew 18:4

110 After the Flood, chap. 4 (see note 7)

111 A man with a tail had men with tails: "Seilenus ... had a tail at the lower part of his back and his descendants also regularly carried this distinguishing mark because of their participation in his nature." (see note 45) Now I highly doubt that this was a functional tail, but probably more like a blob of useless flesh that was transmitted to their offspring.

112 2 Peter 3:3–8 (Scriptures taken from the Holy Bible, New International Version®, NIV®. Copyright © 1973, 1978, 1984 by Biblica, Inc.™ Used by permission of Zondervan. All rights reserved worldwide.)

113 12 Timothy 3:1–9

114 I have had people ask me what part of what I wrote is required for them to inherit eternal life. I'm not sure. I know that the thief on the cross next to Jesus didn't have Jesus expounding to him the history of mankind. I wager that it is much less about the facts you hear about or all of the positions you take. If you come to decide that God used evolution, and you never hear the evidence in this book, it may not even come up when you stand before God. By far, the most important issues are these: 1. We are saved by God, not by anything we do. (Ephesians 2:8) 2. Did you learn to love your neighbor? (Matthew 7:12) If your belief in an old earth brings you to love less, or causes others around you to love less, I believe it will be a problem for you in the end. All false beliefs result in some error, so be careful that you are not wrong.

115 Virgil, "*The Aeneid Book VIII.*" http://www.online-literature.com/virgil/aeneid/8/ (accessed July 15, 2010).

116 Diodorus, book 1 (see note 53), as well as all other quotes in this section until noted otherwise.

117 Hyginus, *Fabulae,* Approx 50 AD.

118 Diodorus Siculus. *The Library of History.* Book 7, 50 BC.

119 Hyginus, *Fabulae,* #54 Liv. Thetis, Approx 50 AD.

120 Hyginus, *Fabulae,* #65 Alcyone, Approx 50 AD.

121 Isaiah 14:12, he falls from heaven. The morning star is Venus, which I have read of Lucifer several places.

122 Hyginus, *Fabulae,* #224 Mortals Who Were Made Immortal, Approx 50 AD.

123 Hyginus, *Fabulae,* #178 Europa, Approx 50 AD.

124 Philo, *On the Eternity of the World.* Chap. XVIII, Online ed. Cornerstone Publications, Approx 30 AD.

125 Philo, *On the Eternity of the World.* Chap. XX, Online ed. Cornerstone Publications, Approx 30 AD.

126 Diodorus, book 2 (see note 38): "... Semiramis [...] when she was informed that the Indian nation was the largest one in the world and likewise possessed both the most extensive and the fairest country, she purposed to make a campaign into India. Stabrobates [... had] many elephants [...] fitted out in an exceedingly splendid fashion [...] For India is a land of unusual beauty, and since it is traversed by many rivers it is supplied with water over its whole area and yields two harvests each year; consequently it has such an abundance of the necessities of life that at all times it favours its inhabitants with a bounteous enjoyment of them. And it is said that because of the favourable climate in those parts the country has never experienced a famine or a destruction of crops." Also "Now India is four-sided in shape and the side which faces east and that which faces south are embraced by the Great Sea,1 while that which faces north is separated by the Emodus range of

mountains from that part of Scythia which is inhabited by the Scythians known as the Sacae; and the fourth side, which is turned toward the west, is marked off by the river known as the Indus, which is the largest of all streams after the Nile." Others have similar descriptions.

127 Strabo, *The Geography,* book 15, Approx. 10 BC

128 Herrnstein, Richard J. and Murray, Charles. *Bell Curve: Intelligence and Class Structure in American Life.* Free Press, January 10, 1996.

129 All quotes this paragraph are from Herodotus (see note 63)

130 "Of all the days in the year, the one which they celebrate most is their birthday." (same passage from Herodotus)

131 Herodotus. *The History of Herodotus.* Book 3. 450 BC.

132 Pliny the Elder. *The Natural History.* Book 7, chapter 16. Approx. 50 AD.

133 Pliny the Elder. *The Natural History.* Book 7, chapter 19. Approx. 50 AD.

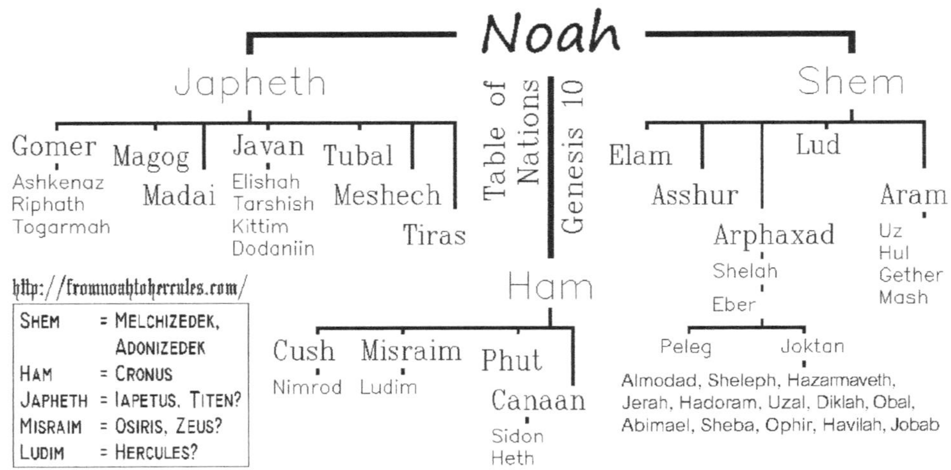
Noah
Japheth
Shem
Ham
Table of Nations
Genesis 10
Gomer
Ashkenaz
Riphath
Togarmah
Magog
Madai
Javan
Elishah
Tarshish
Kittim
Dodaniin
Tubal
Meshech
Tiras
Elam
Asshur
Arphaxad
Shelah
Eber
Peleg
Joktan
Almodad, Sheleph, Hazarmaveth,
Jerah, Hadoram, Uzal, Diklah, Obal,
Abimael, Sheba, Ophir, Havilah, Jobab
Lud
Aram
Uz
Hul
Gether
Mash
Cush
Nimrod
Misraim
Ludim
Phut
Canaan
Sidon
Heth
http://fromnoahtohercules.com/
SHEM = MELCHIZEDEK, ADONIZEDEK
HAM = CRONUS
JAPHETH = IAPETUS, TITEN?
MISRAIM = OSIRIS, ZEUS?
LUDIM = HERCULES?

The Nations of Noah

http://fromnoahtohercules.com/

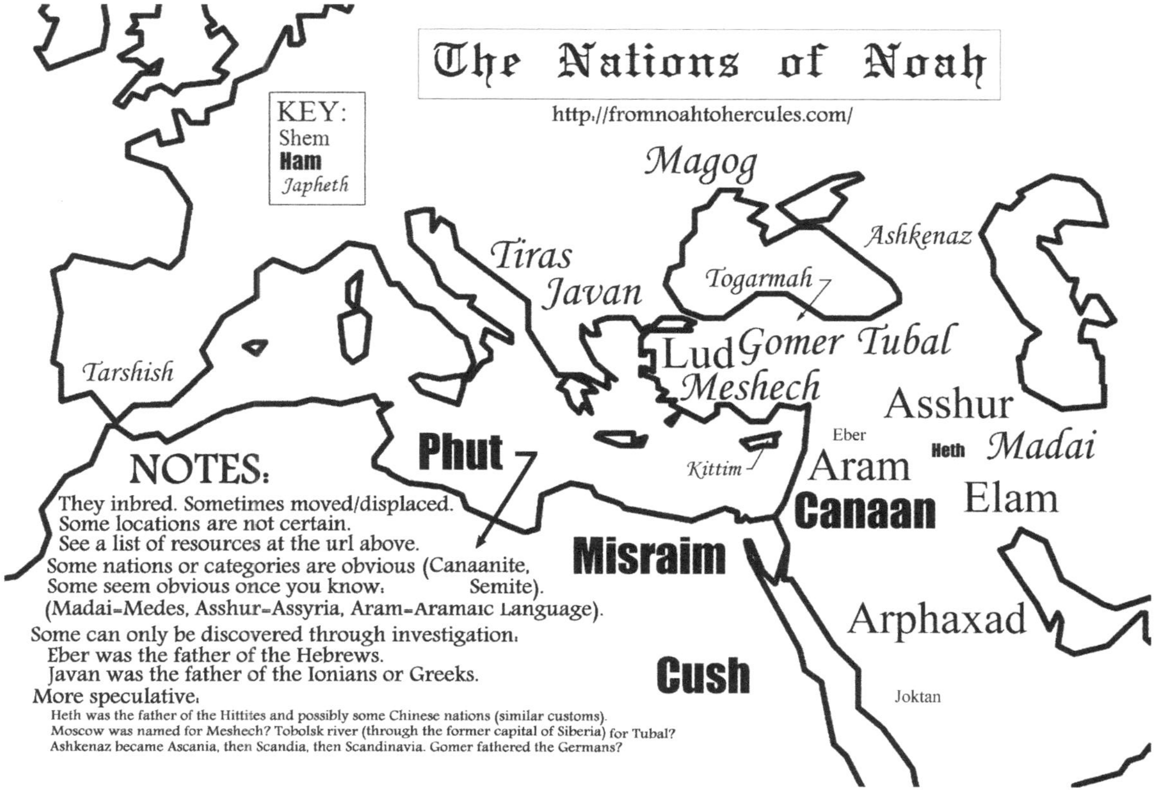

NOTES:

They inbred. Sometimes moved/displaced.
Some locations are not certain.
See a list of resources at the url above.
Some nations or categories are obvious (Canaanite, Semite).
Some seem obvious once you know:
(Madai=Medes, Asshur=Assyria, Aram=Aramaic Language).
Some can only be discovered through investigation:
Eber was the father of the Hebrews.
Javan was the father of the Ionians or Greeks.
More speculative:
Heth was the father of the Hittites and possibly some Chinese nations (similar customs).
Moscow was named for Meshech? Tobolsk river (through the former capital of Siberia) for Tubal?
Ashkenaz became Ascania, then Scandia, then Scandinavia. Gomer fathered the Germans?

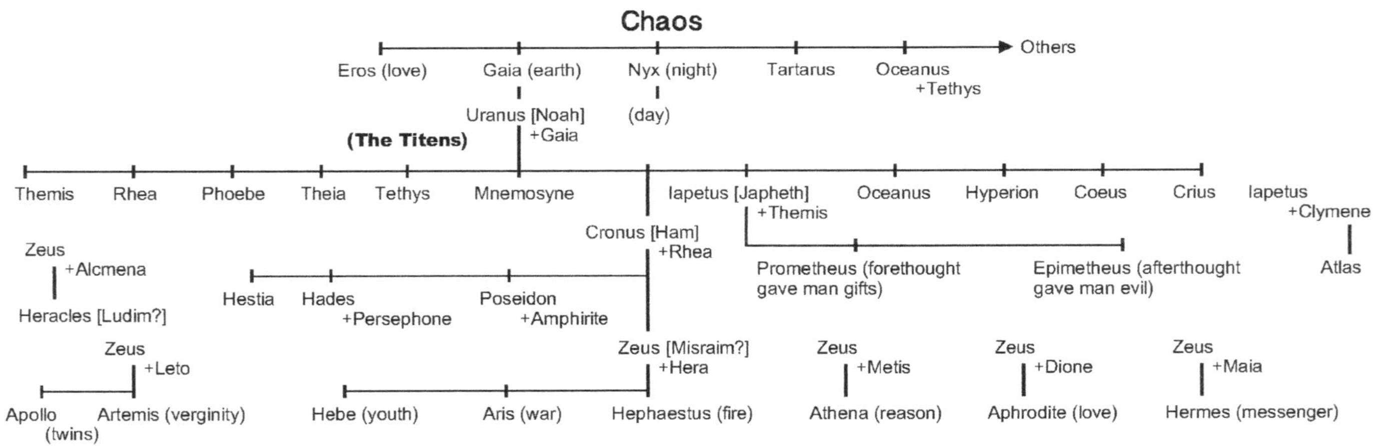

Notes:
Cronus castrated his father; Ham looked upon his father's nakedness.
Ludim might be a varient of Lubim, or Lybia, the nation of Heracles.
Many nations keeping bad records might have made some of these overlap.

Name Chart

Name	Equivalents
Uranus	Noah (Noe) Ianus (Janus) Noeas Xisuthrus Deucalion?
Gaia	Titea (Noah's wife) Vesta Regina sacrorum Gê **
Iapetus	Japheth (Japhet) Atlas?*
Cronus	Ham (Cham) Pan Zoroast Kronos
?	Shem (Sem) Melchisedech (Melchizedek)
Zeus	Misraim? (Aegyptus) Jupiter Zên
Ninus	Nimrod (many varients) Nembroth

* Atlas is the son of Iapetus in most accounts, but given the confused nature of most of what is written, and the absence of anything substantial done by Iapetus, and the account given by Diodorus of the Atlantian history, calling Atlas the son of Uranus who inherited Europe (see my appendix), it does give us pause.

** "Titaea [...] was changed to Gê. [...] Rhea, whom some also named Pandora." (Diodorus, book 3)

Kings of Europe as Given by Lynche

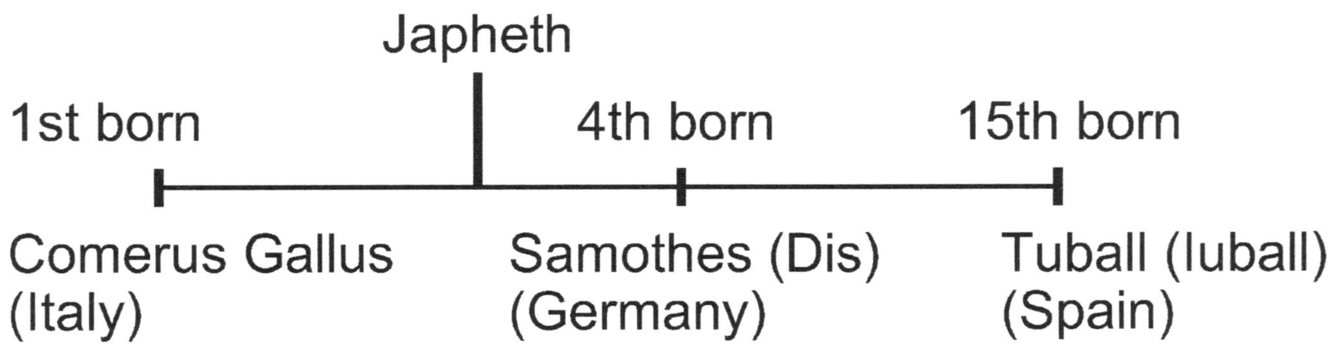

The Account of Osiris as Told by Lynche

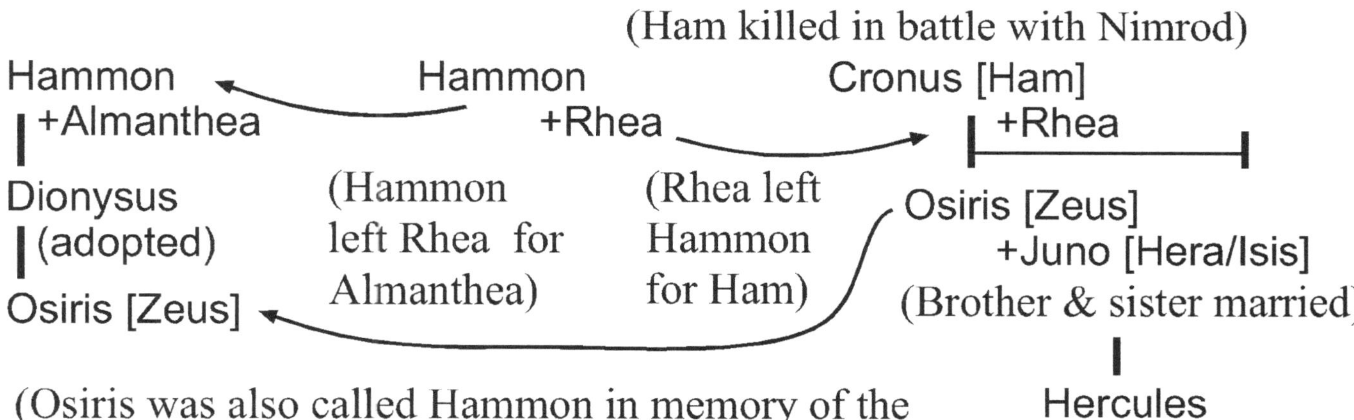

(Osiris was also called Hammon in memory of the adopted grandfather who was killed by Ham, called Olympicus for a teacher who he had in his youth.)

Lightning Source UK Ltd.
Milton Keynes UK
UKOW06f1808131015

260475UK00005B/345/P

9 781617 394287